Contemporary Discourses on Literary Theory

Contemporary Discourses on Literary Theory

Dr. Alka Sharma

OMEGA PUBLICATIONS
New Delhi-110002

OMEGA PUBLICATIONS
4378/4-B JMD House, Ansari Road,
Daryaganj, New Delhi – 110 002
Phone: 23278062 (Off.)
E-mail : omega_publications@yahoo.com

Head Office:
79/23, Laxmi Garden,
Near Satya Jyoti School,
Gurgaon (Haryana)

Price Rs. 850/-

First Published 2023

ISBN : 978-93-94335-31-8

PRINTED IN INDIA

Published by Mahendra Garg for Omega Publications, New Delhi -110 002 and Printed at Tarun Offset Press, New Delhi - 110 053

FOREWORD

Owing to a preponderance of the variety of pedagogical topics on research theories dealt with this catalytic volume titled **"Contemporary Discourses on Literary Theory"** will ultimately be relished by every genre of Linguistic and literary scholastic community. The multi-faceted analytical framework of the book makes it an immensely readable volume that elaborates on the various processes of assimilation. In theme and treatment, every chapter carries an esoteric reflection holding a mirror up to the sparsely delineated issues such as Identity, Geospatial and Digital Humanities, Media and connoisseur ethics, development-oriented planes of communication, Ideological roaming over eco-cultural studies as well as eco-critical investigations, value-centred mediations on post-modern narratives fantasy - fiction etc. Indeed, a section is added exploring English language teaching and the importance of information communication tools in teaching.

Apart from introducing prominent pedagogic linkages that corroborate diverse perspectives such as language, writing, and evaluation -a compact study on the data analysis framework has also been meticulously endeavoured in the volume wholesomely. The author outlines, explores, defines, and draws us into the essence of linguistic struggles with issues regarding environment, ethos, habitats and historicity. The volume throws (casts) an ambient aura on rarely attempted linguistic and pedagogic realms such as the stereotypical faiths and ideologies embedded in the postmodern vis-à-vis postcolonial fiction writing. A syllogistic survey on morality, culture and gender roles that are resplendent in 21st century. Neo-Feminism, New-wave cellulosic parameters has been earnestly decoded and deciphered in the pattern of set evaluation, rendering a brilliant exposition.

Moreover, this book provides pathfinding reasons for avid minds that aspire to sharpen their skills in the arena of audio-visual media and the construction of identity through things as Bill Brown propounded. A punctilious reference has been rendered on eco-critical studies which is the amalgam of literature and environment from the interdisciplinary point of view where all sciences appear tenderised to seek out solutions for global issues that threaten the sustenance of life and longevity of habitats.

The book could surely be estimated as a beacon light of scholastic reason and pedagogical catechism which could in no way be considered a cavalcade for cursory perusal. Dabbling into the profound ocean of innovated and updated ideologies, any ambitious diver could emerge from the depths with pearls and emeralds if attempted in a quintessential and dedicated reading mode as Leopold Bloom had suggested.

Since the topics have intercontinental relevance, the book in every sense stands head and shoulders above its peers regarding the theme, treatment and sterling information it offers. Ardently scanning the book, an ambitious scholar will undoubtedly have the ecstasy of capturing the iridescence of novel ideas regarding creative notions about the methodology and application of linguistic patterns in Post-modern narrative as well as the Post-Covid Digital era narrative where the cornucopia of Media literacy has opened vast portals for flamboyant writing mandates.

The diligent yeomen efforts undertaken by the editor, Dr Alka Sharma in this daring venture of rejuvenating diverse psycholinguistics and pedagogic perspectives aptly deserve laudatory claps and praises since she had sincerely endeavoured to enliven the rarely frequented scholastic realms, which would otherwise have faded into oblivion. My wholehearted cheers for her innovative assay trying to maintain a galaxy of creative and motivational principles radiant on the horizon of pedagogy, by pushing away the clouds of darkness.

- Krishna Kishore
Chief Editor
Anyatha and Otherwise
1062 Robin Court
New Brighton, MN 55113, U.S.A.

ACKNOWLEDGEMENT

It gives me great pleasure to express my profound gratitude to my revered father, Dr. S. B. Dixit, for his unwavering intellectual and emotional support. Without his encouragement and guidance, I would not have attained even the modest standards that this compendium can claim.

I would acknowledge the continual support and vision of Dr. Rajinder Singh, Principal, S.D. College, Ambala Cantt. His dynamism, vision and motivation always inspired me.

I am deeply indebted to Prof. K.K. Sharma, who not only inspired and initiated me into research but also wrote the "Foreword" for this book.

I wholeheartedly appreciate the acumen, passion, and unwavering efforts invested by my colleague, Ms. Jaswinder Kaur, in spearheading the editing of the papers. I am grateful to her for her steadfast support, which was a source of great fortitude for me.

My sincere gratitude goes to all the contributors for their invaluable time and expertise, without which this project would have been an elusive dream.

My dream would not have come to fruition without the unwavering support of my husband, Mr. P. P. Vashisth, and my sons, Satvik and Vishrut, whose presence and perspectives enabled me to bring my project to completion.

Contents

1. Changing Culture and Society Through Indian Advertising Appeals : A Qualitative Analysis

Swetha K.

Abstract: Advertising is a simple tool for marketing. Every media platform has its advertisement department and is dominant among the other departments. This is the reason behind the growth of the advertisement industry in a full-fledged manner over a short period. The role of advertisements is highly inevitable for creating persuasion. This study aims to analyse the transformation of culture and society through these advertising appeals and how it affects stereotypes. Because India has such a large population and cultural diversity, the advertising business has developed a variety of adverts to ensure that they appeal to a wide range of people and persuade others to buy the merchandise by enticing them. The appeals are made in such a way that it has an impact on people's purchase decisions. For that, every advertising agency goes through various stages including psychological for getting the best results by selling their products. So that every advertisement mends to appeal to the audience. This study tries to bring light to Indian advertising appeals and how it is affected culture and society.

Keywords: Advertising appeals, Culture and Society, Advertisements, Stereotypes, Marketing Strategy, Brand awareness, Culture diversity, small-scale business

Introduction: Advertising is one of the operative and systematic ways of outbound media. Advertisements help to disseminate their message through multiple media platforms, especially television, radio, and social media. But the major function lies down with the increase of profit and revenue of the company. Also, it has become the most important commercial activity in this modern competitive era. Every advertisement appeal is the reason for consumers to choose the product. Companies spend a large amount of time and money to produce an appealing advertisement. Consumers are bombarded with many types of advertisements.to attract the audience there should be something more than tangible. This can only do by advertising appeals. If a customer is interested in a product, it can be mainly because of the advertising appeal which they are spreading through their advertisements. Earlier many of the companies were only focused into rational appeal mode but later they understood that emotional appeal gives more attention among the consumers. So, the trend is now gradually shifting from rational appeal to emotional appeal. Companies have started to using emotional elements in their advertisements to create a powerful impact in the minds of consumers. This led to the change in the buying behaviour of a consumer.

Advertising in this 21st century is highly demanding. Because the role of advertising is vital in developing small-scale businesses and bringing a competitive mind towards other companies. The advertising and marketing industry continuously developing in terms of market size, quality of the product and content. With a successful advertising campaign, a company can grow further. Also, it is very needed for any advertisement to consider social issues by using technological advancements to create more creative content. Many advertising critics discussed that advertising has a great impact on consumerism and cultural values. They also believe that advertisers promote superficial consumerism by creating "false consciousness and "manipulate the symbols that serve as the social fabric of human association (Wharton, 2013)

Significance of the study

This study is important due to the change in advertisements in the industry. The effects of advertisements are no longer limited, they can both positively and negatively impact society depending upon the content of the message and how it is decoded with the values, norms and cultures of the society. Language is also a medium to spread social values. Advertisers are always concern about the non-verbal and verbal expressions which they used. In sum, companies around the world are integrating social responsibilities in their advertisements as well as their overall business. This enhances the relationship between targeted audience and the company. Commercial advertisements are one step forward to use social relevant issues in their advertisements. Since the advertisement patterns are changing which is also leading the change of culture and society. Changes in the buying behaviour among the consumers is the real example of the change in society. So, this study is relevant because advertisements can shape the perception of the society.

Research Methodology

Qualitative analysis was employed in this study to understand the role advertising plays in shaping the cultural value. The historical-analytical technique is used here, with both primary and secondary sources. A desk review of the policy document, in-depth interviews, researches, and other documents included in all parts of the article. The analysis part supported with some kinds of literature of research. A study on advertisements was conducted to examine how culture and society is shaped through advertisements. This particular study focused on primary source as consumers as well as some documents and media platforms mainly social media as my secondary source to know the social responsibilities in the advertisements. Used secondary materials to get an understanding the consumer behaviour. Also collected secondary materials to know the change in the perspective of people through advertising appeals. Primary data mainly focused on in-depth interviews with a semi-structured questionnaire of around 15 open ended questions. In-depth interviews were mainly collected to analyse the depiction of different stimuli in advertisements such as celebrity endorsements, humour, language, religion, clothing, patriotism, festivity and lifestyle influence the culture of the consumers. Aspects like friendship, relationships, family and environment were also studied here. Data collected by filtering contents according to advertising appeals such as contemporary advertisements portrayed social issues, the role of advertisements in changing social perception, and the change in consumer behaviour pattern.

Objectives of the study

- To examine the influence of culture, socioeconomic factors on consumer behaviour pattern towards advertisements.
- To analyse the consumer experience of ad pattern
- To examine the change in culture and society by advertising appeals
- To understand Indian advertisements are changing consumer's culture

Review of literature

Many studies say that advertising plays a vital role in reflecting communities shared values and shaping societies. For example, looking at how broad communications could be used to expressly promote a societal transformation that crippled societies and replaced their culture with a pseudo-culture. The pseudo-culture theory of Adorno was used to investigate how political ideologies can affect societal transformation through mass-mediated advertisement images. For a span of 48 years, the researchers used semiotic and content analysis to examine print advertisements. The researchers discovered five key features that underpin the emergence of pseudo-cultures and the marketing methods that promote them. It also identified four key tools for creating, promoting, and eradicating pseudo-cultures, as well as how pseudo-cultures might be formed, promoted, and eradicated (Yazdanparast, 2018).

The major elements that can affect the appeal of a social media advertisement, according to a study conducted by Noel JK, are changes made to the ad's content, user engagement values linked with the ad, and user-generated comments (UGCs) related to the ad. Noel looked into the popularity of beer ads on Facebook and discovered that it is mostly influenced by the content of the ads. When non-compliant advertising makes extensive use of emotional appeal, the advertisement is more likely to be recalled and impact future drinking occasions (Noel, 2018).

Kotler (1997) found out that the theme of an advertisement is advertising appeal. Advertisers must provide some driving force to the message in order for the audience to receive it. The appeal is the motivating force behind this. Every commercial appeal reflects an allure that piques the interest of consumers. He also distinguished between intellectual and emotional appeals in advertising. Advertisers frequently utilise rational and emotional appeal in their advertising to influence public behaviour in order to suit the diverse requirements of their targeted audience. Suppliers employ a psychologically motivating force to increase consumers' desire and action for purchase while delivering broadcasting signals to transform receivers' notions of the goods, according to Schiffman and Kanuk (2007). As a result, advertising appeal is used to draw consumers' attention, modify their perceptions of a product, and influence them emotionally regardg a certain goods or services.

Su Jiangli indicated after studying American movie trailers, car ads, and fast-food chain advertisements that American companies in China not only promote their goods or services, but also advertise American culture, values, and way of life through advertising, and that this has an impact on Chinese teenagers and the middle class. Jiangli believes they are an important component of American soft power and that they can effectively meet the three pillars of public diplomacy: daily communication, strategic communication, and long-term relationship building. Furthermore, Jiangli claim that they have the potential to shift the abstract soft power of cultural values towards something more observable, and that their influence is widespread since they can effectively affect the lives of Chinese people. This could pose a challenge to preserving traditional Chinese culture and values. (2015, Jiangli).

Using semiotic and rhetoric analysis, N. Anido Freire examined commercials for two luxury firms that exhibit identification ideals of luxury. The study determined the semic depth of discursive content in each luxury brand's symbolic imagery and identity narratives, as well as their consequences. According to Freire, the existence and success of large luxury houses lies in the worldwide coherence they employ in terms of production, goods, storytelling, and advertising, which maintains their brand image and attracts more devoted clients (Freire,2014).

When emotional appeals are exploited in advertising, the product's consumption pattern is very pleasant. Soap commercials frequently employ sex appeal. The audience is drawn in by the arousal of desire, which ultimately aids in the sale of the commodity. Sex appeal is mostly used to appeal to the opposite gender, whether masculine or feminine (Wright, 2000). According to Bradley (1995), sex appeal is occasionally regard as a crime depending on the culture and country, but it is allowed in society if the sex appeal is not vulgar. Love appeal is used in perfumes and cosmetics. These appeals are more commonly employed by the younger generation.

Case studies

Ariel's #sharetheload

Ariel has succeeded to create a social asset, #ShareTheLoad, by combining their brand identity with an ideology of their beliefs, resulting in an endeavour that goes much further than just digital marketing. #ShareTheLoad has become the brand's implicit identity, and it also managed to generate some goodwill with its campaign, which was a little step toward change involving only laundry. "Can't guys do laundry?" was a simple concept that rang through people's heads in a way, and it was made important on a very social level. An idea that was discussed on a global scale after the campaign was launched in India, Pakistan, Bangladesh, and Sri Lanka, but the thought soared even higher when it went viral in 22 nations and 16 languages. #ShareTheLoad did not boast of ideas in its substance, but it did beautifully highlight one facet of gender equality. Ariel presented an issue before it became a trend on social media by businesses, and it seemed to fit with their content for an audience who might empathise with the notion and be encouraged to consider it.

Jabong: Be You

This much-discussed slick ad film, created in association with Bates CHI & Partners by London-based creative and art director Harvey B Brown, features gorgeous views of men and women making extreme fashion statements. Models of all body kinds and races swish about in sequins and denim, guys with heavy kohl-lined lids and pigtails offer the camera smouldering glares, ladies pout with green lipstick, and men with heavy kohl-lined lids and pigtails give the camera sultry glares. You don't have to call me pretty, you don't deserve my sympathy, I'm just me, the songs say. Asheesh Malhotra, President, Head of Mumbai and Delhi, Bates CHI & Partners, argues how fashion in India is misinterpreted and equated to "bright lovely clothing" being worn on "chiselled bodies." According to him, the purpose of the campaign was to refocus the debate on fashion, pushing beyond the fabric to speak to those who wanted to be trendy while remaining confident and comfortable rather than being imprisoned by trends. He told "The team developed a campaign that is rule-bending but not preachy."

The campaign's central message is about valuing oneself and

embarking on one's own personal journey, as well as being honest to oneself, feeling good, and confidently expressing oneself. The commercial's lively and upbeat 130-second music score is a youthful mix of melody, tempo, and meaningful lyrics. The song's visualisation emits a sense of independence, unique journey, and optimism that the company has cultivated over the years through its services.

Dove India: Let's Break the Rules of Beauty

Dove has a global reputation in the women's cosmetics sector for encouraging the respect of varying standards of beauty, and their latest campaign in India is no exception. In a country as anthropologically diverse as India, this advertisement asks why there is only one ideal of female beauty. In a country with 631 million women, 29 states, and 22 languages, a new Dove study found that 76 percent of Indian women believe it is necessary to satisfy specific beauty standards in today's culture. Dove's latest campaign, "Let's Break the Rules of Beauty," reinterpreted existing beauty standards and inspired India to embrace its diversity in beauty with a film shot with 85 women across India. Dove's latest campaign encourages women to cherish their individual characteristics as much as established stereotypes. Pan Nalin, an Indian film director, screenwriter, and documentary maker, shot the film "Let's Break the Rules of Beauty," which features "Real Women" from various Indian states. Eighty-five women were captured in their own avatars, each promoting their own definition of beauty.

Bhima Jewellery's Pure as Love

The film depicts a transgender woman's journey and the normalcy that surrounds her. The commercial depicts not only her path to being who she is, but also her family's love and acceptance of their child. They cast a real transgender person because they wanted to keep the authenticity. Moreover, they poured justice to the cause, person as well as to the community. In India, giving jewellery is an ingrained tradition and in a way, it's a form of giving someone a blessing. People don't just buy jewellery; it's collected over a period of time. It also comes with a connotation of acceptance too.

It's a journey that has one key component: accepting parents. Instead of the normal fear and rejection that greets those who learn their gender is different than their birth-assigned one, the transwoman here is greeted with a faint but powerful undercurrent of love and acceptance. Each little item contributes to the metamorphosis, from the women bicycle sitting in the bedroom to the golden anklets presented by the father to the mother waiting patiently while her son/daughter gets her ears pierced. The picture also succeeds because it is understated. There is no theatrics, tears, or preaching in this film. Each ephemeral frame is densely filled with meaning, but in a subtle way. Everything is mined for meaning by the filmmaker, Bharat Sikka, from the pink of the ice-cream stand to the rainbow hues of the bubbles she blows on the beach to the attentive stroking of the beard in the initial moments, yet he does it so gently that it blends in with the surroundings. Most significantly, both in her prior and current incarnations, the transwoman emerges with dignity intact. Avoiding the customary images of humiliation and transphobia may appear idealistic, and it is, but it accomplishes a critical goal: it normalises and wholesomely depicts the trans body, making it as common as a hetero body. More importantly, it demonstrates a different way of reacting to a trans person. It has the capacity to become more appetising when wrapped in the consumerist glitter of gold and jewellery, rather than when presented in the brown-paper packaging of homilies.

Conclusion

Today, in this modern world the internet as well as television changed the communication paradigm and it has no longer difficult to reach the majority of the society. So that advertisements play a vital role in the changing behaviour of consumers. Advertisement has emerged as a powerful weapon to convince consumers to adopt change even in their social culture. Through that, each company brands their identity. The brands taken as case studies had both rational and emotional appeal in their advertisements. They come up with most of the relevant social issues of that particular time and grabbed the attention of the society. These advertisements even were part of a social change. Especially in the so-called gender roles and stereotypes. As a result, the companies sell grab the consumer's attention and sell their products more by incorporating with socially relevant themes. Ultimately, the aim of an advertisement is to sell their product. By spreading those appeals through advertisements, the companies try to keep the brand name in the minds of consumers. All these appeals are finally leading to the shift of a social change and change in cultural patterns of the society. So, advertisements have a significant role in revamping the social structure of a society.

Works cited:

Abokhoza Reneh, Sherehan Hamdalla Mohamed, Dr. Sumit Narula. "How Advertising Reflect Culture and Values: A Qualitative Analysis Study." Journal of Content, Community & Communication, Amity School of Communication (2019)

Arora, Mnish "Impact of Advertising on Indian Society to Improve Awareness with Special Reference to Social Advertisement." Interdisciplinary Journal of Contemporary Research, Vol. 6, No. 1 (January 2019)

Kotler, Philip. (2000). Marketing Management. 10th Ed. New York: Free Press.

Kumar, Keval J. "Mass Communication in India." Jaico Publishing House, 2013.

Mishra, Anil. "Indian Perspective about Advertising Appeal." International Journal for Marketing Studies (2019)

Bhagat, Neha. "Emerging trend of Emotional Appeal in Indian Television Advertising." IOSR Journal of Humanities and Social Science (IOSR-JHSS) 22.8 (2017): 27-30.

Shaju, P P. "Corporate Communication and Advertising". Calicut University Central Co-Operative Stores Ltd., 2016.
Schiffman LG, Kanuk LL. "Consumer Behaviour." Pearson Education International Press. (2007)

2. Concept of Marriage in Eighteenth-Century Literature

Dr Jaideep Chauhan

Abstract: Eighteenth-century literature seems to have championed the cause of women seeking equality and liberty. In contemporary society, their condition was far from satisfactory. Under the influence of the changed political climate during Charles II's regime and the advent of new scientific thinking, the comedy of the period started challenging the age-old notions and conventions regarding man-woman relationships. It tried to show the possibilities of gaining more equality and liberty than what was hitherto allowed to them. And in this respect Restoration Comedy seems to be ahead of its time. Even the immorality and adulterous propensities of women in the Comedy can be interpreted in the light of this idea: its espousal of women's cause- a revolt against the age-old dogmas and beliefs and the quest for existence.

Keywords: Marriage, Separation, Divorce, Unhappy, Harmony, Liberty, Equality

Before studying the literature of the time, it is worthwhile to have the historical perspective of the man-woman relationship. Conventionally, marriages were arranged by parents without taking into account the inclinations of the people concerned. In the male-dominated society, there was no scope for a woman to dissent from the marriage alliance which was, by and large, prompted by the mercenary motives of the parents. The mercenary marriage of marriage-de-convenience totally neglected the protestant ideal of love, and thereby it generated unrest among the youth. An alternative to the evils of marriage-de-convenience was found in marrying secretly. Some of the churches viz. Convent Garden Church, St. Pancras, Duke's Place etc. were notorious for clandestine marriages. Comedy of the time frequently alludes to such churches and marriages.

Once married, either of the spouse, especially a woman, had no release from the marriage bonds except in the case of child marriage, fraud, bigamy etc. A wife could get only some financial relief such as a separate maintenance allowance in the case of bigamy. The Canon Law showed no clemency to a wife committing adultery. Adulterous women were punished by the ecclesiastical courts and sometimes were even burnt alive. The Civil Marriage Act of 1653 also gave no relief to an unhappily married woman. Although it transferred jurisdiction over marriage disputes from the religious courts to the Civil Courts, it did not allow women to seek justice. Women, therefore, started objecting to male dominance and double standard of behaviour allowed by the society. Restoration Comedy joins their banner.

A shift in the contemporary matrimonial laws also contributed to the changing attitude towards husband-wife relationship and thus it provided the playwrights with ample material for marital discord plots. The Civil Marriage Act by its transference of jurisdiction shattered religious sanctity of matrimony as an alliance made in heaven. The Act considered marriage as a man-made contract latent with the possibility of annulment which it had vested with the Parliament. For a divorce decree, the separation petition had to be filed in and granted by the ecclesiastical courts. However, obtaining a separate petition from the religious courts was a very long, expensive and scandalous venture which only men could undertake for; the Act was silent over a woman's right to testify against her husband. Nevertheless, the very idea of separation seems to have created climate congenial to remedying the ills of unhappy marriages.

The Duke of Norfolk, who had obtained separation by mutual

consent in 1685 and had to fight a long legal battle before he could get a Parliamentary divorce in 1700 was the first instance of legally ending the miseries of an unhappy marriage. His was an exceptional case, for; money and personal influence played a significant role in getting him released from the marriage contract. Again in 1701 two persons, Sir John Dillon and a London grocer, Ralph Rox, could get their marriages dissolved after obtaining separation from the Doctors' Commons, the religious court of England. In short, by the end of the seventeenth century the history of matrimonial laws evinced proclivity in favour of separation and divorce as a possible release from unhappy marriage bonds.

The contemporary writers and philosophers also contributed to finding a remedy to the evils of marriage. Locke in The Second Treatise describes marriage as voluntary contract that provides a wife, "the full and free possession of what by contract is her peculiar right." He further allows her liberty to separate from her husband "where natural rights, or their contract allows it". Milton too crusaded against the double standard of behaviour permitted by the contemporary matrimonial laws. In The Doctrine and Discipline of Divorce which he had tabled before the Parliament in 1643 - he avers:

> Marriage is a cov'nant the very being whereof consists, not in a forc'd cohabitation and counterfeit performance of duties, but in unfained love and peace.

He considers mismatched alliances unnatural and destructive. He maintains that "harmony of the homogenous and divorce of the unlike elements is the law of nature". The thrust of his argument is that "to part from an unjust man is happiness, and no injury to be lamented". The social perspective and the views of the thinkers given hitherto can further a better understanding of the issue handled by the contemporary comedy. It questioned the double standard of behaviour and revolted against male dominance. Maria, the champion of equality, in Fletcher's *The Woman's Prize, or, The Tamer Tam'd* (1633) corroborates:

> Take two small drops of water, equal weigh'd Tel me which is the heaviest, and which ought First to descend in duty?

Woman is no longer supposed to have been created from man's ribs. Subjugation and subordination of women is decried in comedy. It ushered her into a new liberated world and endowed her with equal wit and qualities of the head and heart. The comedy also ridiculed marriage alliances contracted for mercenary gains only. Revolting against the restrictive authority of the parents, person of one's choice and entertaining marrying clandestinely the gallants and cuckolding also seem to be approved redress to the ills of marriage alliances contracted with an eye, not on love, but on wealth. This is decried by Lucinda in Sir Richard Steele's comedy, *The Conscious Lovers* (1722):

> What is the world come to? No shame left! To be bartered for like beasts of the fields, and that in such an instance as coming together to an entire familiarity and union of soul and body. Oh! And this without being so much as well-wishers to each other but for increase of fortune.

Palamede, the young spokesman of young lovers, in Dryden's Marriage a-la-Mode (1671) disparages marriage-de-convenience when he presents his predicament before his friend

What marriage means conventionally to a woman is lashed by Lucinda in *The Conscious Lovers,* thus:

> Mamma says the first time you see your husband should be at that instant he is made so, when your father with the help of the Minister gives you to him, then you are to observe and take notice of him, because then you are to obey him.

Happolita in William Wycherley's *The Gentleman Dancing Master* (1672) denounces marriadge-de-convenience for she thinks:

> Fathers seldom choose well and I will no more take my father's choice in a husband than I would in a gown or a suit of knots....

She appears to be the spokesman of the younger generation that considers love as the only foundation of happy marriage. She avers:

> The match soon made is happy still,
> For only lover has there to do;
> Let no one marry against her will,
> But stand-off, when her parents woo.

Belinda in Vanbrugh's *The Provok'd Wife* (1697) prefers to marry for love even a poor younger brother. So is Leanthe in Farquhar's *Love and a Battle* (1698) determined to marry a poor extravagant rake. Nevertheless, most of the lovers in Restoration comedy try and test each other's constancy. Their love is neither self-annihilation of the platonic love of heroic drama, nor mere rovings of the libertines but is a quest for the right companionship. Once the lover's sincerity is established, the quest for the compatible companion is over, they welcome matrimonial bonds only after each agrees to the provisos the other has. Mirabel and Millamant in The Way of the World are examples of such a quest.

People who marry for reasons other than love are ridiculed in marital discord plots. Right from Etherege's Lady Cockwood in *She Wou'd if She Cou'd* (1667) to Mrs. Sullen in Farquhar's *The Beaux Stratagem* (1707) there are a host of unhappy women who show how fortune and status are acquired at the cost of domestic felicity. Lady Cockwood has earned a title but is married to a fool, and so are Lady Fidget and Lady Jasper in Wycherley's *The Country Wife* (1675). In the same play Margery Pinchwife is married to a foolish jealous husband. Laetitia, a young beautiful girl is married to a puritan old man, Fondlewife in Congreve's *The Old Bachelor* (1693). Similarly Elvira, a young beautiful daughter of the nobility is married to an old miserly tyrant, Don Diego in Dryden's *The Spanish Friar* (1680) etc. In *The Provok'd Wife,* Lady Brute marries Lord Brute for money and in Farquhar's The

Beaux Stratagem Mrs. Sullen marries for 'protection' and 'happiness' and both suffer miserably. The common thread among such mismatched couples is absence of love and marital bliss. Their marriages have badly failed. It is their example that makes Lucia in *Shadwell's Epsom Wells* (1672) say, "see, what matrimony comes to, or makes Millamant in *The Way of the World* apprehensive of:

> if Mirabel should not make a good husband, I am a
> lost thing; - for I find I love him violently.

No wonder women find marriage vows null and void under the present conventions and in the world of extreme libertinism and double standards of behaviour. Revolt is a natural consequence indeed. Doralice in Dryden's Marriage a-la-Mode rightly does argue the futility of cohabitation forced by old values and traditions. Her objection:

> Why should a foolish vow,
> which long ago was made,
> Oblige us to each other now,
> when passion is decay'd?

Though quite logical is not justifiable in her case since she is happily married to Rhodophil. No doubt, her attempt to seek complete liberty after the manner of Hobbesian state of Nature is rendered unsuccessful by the Muse. The play depicts that there should be only one code of conduct for both the spouses. Nevertheless, the play has potent for a revolt that many an unhappy wife resorts to.

Many of the victims of unhappy alliances and double standard of behaviour seem to justify seeking extra-marital bliss that appears quite in keeping with the moral code operative in Charles II's Court. Lady Fidget in *The Country Wife* questions her husband's tyranny thus:

> Why should our damn'd tyrants oblige us to live,
> On the pittance of Pleasures which they only give.

Lady Brute, dissatisfied with her married life is allowed to defend her case in political terms:

> But he has n't kept his words. Why then I'm absolv'd from mine. Aye, that seems clear to me. The Argument is good between the king and the people, why not between the Husband and Wife?

Lady Wronglove in *Cibber's The Lady's Last Stake; or The Wife's Resentment* (1708) expresses her discontent thus:

> Sure, men think that wives are stocks or stones, without all sense of injuries or only born and bound to bear them.

Comedy of the period is evidence that neither adultery, even as a revolt, nor keeping appearance and making pretensions to virtue and honour will assuage the surging dissatisfaction and miseries of unhappy marriages. Lady Cockwood, Lady Jasper, Lady Plyant and Lady Foresight might try their best to keep appearances of loving wives, their actions belie their words and their discontent can be seen and felt through the veneer of their appearances.

Not all the women seeking release from unhappy marriage bonds pleasure through gallants are presented triumphant. Elvira, a virtuous young girl of a respectable family is married to Gomez, the old tyrant in *The Spanish Fariar*. She tries to escape from her captivity but Dryden does not provide her any release whatsoever. Mrs. Fribble and Mrs. Bisket, the citizen wives in Shadwell's Epsom Wells are doomed to lead a most miserable life in spite of their attempts to revolt against their cruel husbands. Perhaps, Dryden and Shadwell dared not violate the middle-class morality and annoy the emerging bourgeoise among their audience.

However, the unhappy wives seeking redress through adultery are made either to revert to positive norms or to seek separation through mutual consent. In the last decades of the seventeenth century the desire of the miserable wives to seek happiness extramarital way is thwarted by the playwrights. The adulterous inclinations of the unhappy wives are ascribed to their avowed motives of reclaiming their errant husbands by rousing their jealousy. The libertine husbands are made to realise the havoc they cause to their domestic life, and repent, though in the V Act conversion scene, and revert to positive norms. Amanda in Vanbrugh's *Relapse* (1968) makes Lord Loveless realise the worth of conjugal fidelity through her gallant, Worthy. Lady Brute in *The Provok'd Wife* also entertains gallants in order to reclaim Lord Brute but Vanbrugh like Dryden fails to provide succour to a miserable wife. Mrs. Sullen's efforts in The Beaux Stratagem to reclaim Lord Sullen fail badly. Nevertheless, Farquhar disburses justice to her by allowing her to separate with mutual consent.

Some of the aforesaid bold strokes of the playwrights present before the audience the possible direction of change; the socially acceptable remedy to unhappy wives. The comedies elucidate that in the absence of a flexible divorce procedure only mutual consent for separation could alleviate litigation hardships and miseries thereof. Mrs. Sullen in Miltonic strain defends divorce when she argues her point with her sister-in-law, Dorinda:

> O sister, casual violation is a transient injury, and may possibly be repair'd, but can radical hatred be ever reconcil'd? - No, no, sister, Nature is the first law giver, and when she has set tempers opposite, not all the golden links of wedlock, nor Iron Manacles of Law can keep 'em fast.

Lady Brute's marriage like that of Mrs. Sullen has also come to nothing. She too wants to seek divorce and discusses her predicament with her niece, Belinda:

> I know according to the strict statute law of Religion, I should do wrong; But if there were a Court of Chancery in Heaven, I'm sure I shou'd cast him.

Lady Brute also tries in vain to rouse her husband's jealousy by planning love intrigues. Finally, she seeks separation. Vanbrugh's sympathy for the wronged wife is voiced in his defence of her intrigue in The Short Vindication. He supports her behaviour against the husband, for it is instructive. He says:

> though his ill usage of her does not justify her

intrigues, her intriguing upon his ill-usage, may be a caution for some.

Nevertheless, Vanbrugh does not grant her separation by mutual consent which seems evidence of Vanbrugh's avoidance of annoyance to the moralists and the rising citizen class. On the other hand, Farquhar (himself the victim of a tricked marriage) advocates separation in *The Beaux Stratagem.* Mrs. Sullen and Squire Sullen agree on no other point but separation and Farquhar makes them consent mutually to separate. Their attempt is highly praised by her gallant, Archer:

Both happy in their several states we find,
Those parted by consent, and those conjoined.
Consent, if mutual, saves the lawyer's fee -
Consent is law enough to set you free.

Shadwell too had resolved this problem in Epsom Wells long before Farquhar attempted it in The Beaux Stratagem. The gulf between the Sullens is caused by a clash of temperaments but in Epsom Wells, Mr. Woodly, like Sir John Brute, provokes his wife with his libertine ways and brutish behaviour. Mrs. Woodly is so miserable that she wishes him dead at the hands of her gallant:

If he kills Bevil, I am reveng'd, if he kills him, he rids me of the worst Husband for my humour in Christendom.

In a most comic proviso scene they consent to separate and celebrate it like their wedding as Mr. Woodly puts it:

To show you, that there was never yet so decent a divorce, I have fiddles to play at it as they used to do at weddings.

Mr. Woodly lauds the new approach to matrimonial disputes:

Marriage that does the hearts and will unite,
Is the best state of pleasure and delight;
But when man and wife no longer each other please,
They may at least like us each other ease.

Not all the playwrights, however, support separation by mutual consent, they have a different solution to this problem. Colley Cibber, in Love's Last Shift (1696) presents Amanda, a virtuous wife in distress. Her poignant tears fill the husband with remorse in the fifth-act reformation scene meant to warm the hearts of the moralists. Her virtue triumphs in awakening the latent good in him and he pledges conjugal fidelity which he extols in his final speech:

> And sure the nearest to the joys above,
> Is the chaste rapture of a virtuous love.

In another popular comedy, *The Careless Husband* (1704), Cibber again presents reconciliation as a remedy to unhappy spouses believing in the fact that man by nature is good and reclaimable. Lady Easy, a virtuous wife, is married to Sir Charles Easy, a Libertine rake. Instead of exposing him, she patiently awakens his conscience by putting her scarf over his head lest he should catch cold. Not many unhappy wives do introspect like Lady Easy:

> And duty, too, forbids me to insult Where I have vowed obedience, Perhaps the faults in me, and nature has not formed Me with the thousand little requisites that warm the heart to love.

She knows that continual jealousy and negative ways on her part will rather fix her husband's aversion; it is only virtue and patience that can redeem him. Filled with remorse and penitence he reverts to positive values.

In situations where both the spouses are responsible for unhappiness, Cibber provides a mentor who by gently counselling brings peace and harmony between them. *Lady Wrong Love and Lord Wrong Love in The Lady's Last Stake,* or, *The Wife's Resentment* (1708) are no better than the Woodlys but Sir Friendly Moral advises Lady Wrong Love to lure her husband with "soft affections" and asks Lord Wrong Love to think of the "long-watched, restless hours she has already endured" on account of his misdoings. Both realise their mistakes, repent and are reconciled.

The presentation of amicability, harmony and reconciliation in such sentimental comedies was in consonance with the predominant middle class sensibilities craving for the tenets of Christianity discernible in The Tatler, The Spectator, and the periodicals of Steele and Addison. In cases where only separation could resolve the marital disputes, mutual consent was supported.

Whatever be the situation, comedy of this era approached marital disputes from women's point of view since they were the weaker sex and required pioneers to fight for them. Marriage laws in England did not consider them equal to the other sex. Even Lord Harwicke's Act of 1754, seeking to restrict informal marriage ceremonies and annulment, was silent on the miseries of the unhappily married women. The credit goes to the Restoration Society and comedy for making women voice their dissatisfaction and fight for equality and liberty. The battle was won when in 1801, Mrs. Addison got a divorce decree against her husband. It was then that the voice of Lady Wrong Love was taken note of :

> For if the husband's violation of his marriage-vow is in itself so foul an injury, whence is it that the law is so sparing in its redress? ... If she offends, the crime is unpardonable, yet if injur'd, has no right to compensation, it may be usual this, but sure 'tis unnatural.

Works Cited:

Aliman, G.S. Matrimonial Law and the Materials of Restoration Comedy. Wallingford, 1942.

Smith, J.H. The Gay Couple in Restoration Comedy. Harvard University Press, reprint 2014.

Scouten, A.H. Restoration and Eighteenth Century Drama. Macmillan, 1980.

Visiak, E.H. Milton: Complete Poetry and Selected Prose. The Nonesuch Press, 1964.

3. A Study of Cultural Disintegration in the American Middle-Class Society in the Selected Novels of John Updike

Dr. Anshu Chaudhary

Abstract: John Hoyer Updike has been a renowned figure on the American literary scene since 1959. He is a short story writer, poet, playwright, essayist and critic but it is as a novelist that he is chiefly known. His novels like Rabbit Tetralogy, Couples, Marry Me etc. were such accurate portraits of fifties and sixties American culture that they quickly earned their author his reputation as the novelist of his times. Each of these novels detail the marital tensions, sexual escapades, personal betrayals, professional disappointments and spiritual crises that reflect changing attitudes about sexual behaviour, relationships between men and women, and, most importantly, religious belief in contemporary society. This paper is an attempt to discuss the cultural disintegration of American middle class society with reference to the two of his select novels -*Rabbit, Run* (1960) and *Rabbit Redux* (1971). The domestic reality of suburban, middle-class American life is the focus of Updike's novels of 60s and 70s, including Rabbit, Run and Rabbit Redux. The interminable boredom of the well-to-do middle class is a primary topic in Updike's stories.

Keywords: Moral dilemma, American dream, Marital tensions, Spiritual Dilemma, Contemporary society.

Introduction: In modern literature a richer and more varied inner life is opened up to the readers. The sense of personality is deepened. Modern writers explore the hidden recesses of human nature, reproduce the rarer and more abnormal states of feeling, which has deepened the nature of complexity and ambiguity in the characters and has heightened the moral dilemma of the protagonists' and the reader's dilemma as well.

Because of this focus on the human nature in modern literature the moral element of characters or ethos has become an important study. Ethos is a Greek word meaning "character" that is used to describe the guiding beliefs or ideals that characterize an individual, community, nation, or ideology ("Ethos"). Ethos refers to the spirit which motivates the ideas and customs. An individual in some way or the other is always influenced by the social, economic, and political milieu of his times.

In his seminal work *Poetics*, Aristotle has used two words Ethos and Dionoia which are the two aspects or elements that constitute the character of a living person. Character in its most comprehensive sense is made up of both these elements. Ethos is the moral element, the moral position, and Dionoia is the thought, the intellectual element, which determines all rational conduct, and through which the moral self of a person finds outward expression. In drama as in life, both thought and moral bent of a person reveal themselves in his speeches and in his actions. When we focus on the Ethos, we think of the environment in which the story is written- the intellectual climate, the cultural settings, the customs, the manners relevant to the story which makes it more comprehensive and successful in evoking the desired emotions and feelings in the readers in every age and milieu.

John Updike as a social chronicler has depicted his major themes of domesticity, religion and Americanness by knitting them with the political, economic and social changes of his times. Since the protagonists in Updike's fiction represent the American everyman, therefore, their own thought process- intellectual and moral element represent national ethos. The American Dream is a national ethos of the United States, a set of ideals in which freedom includes the opportunity for prosperity and success, and an upward social mobility achieved through hard work. The Dream, "includes the opportunity for one's children to grow up and receive a good education and career without artificial barriers. It is the opportunity to make individual choices without the prior restrictions that limit people according to their class, caste, religion or ethnicity ("American Dream").

In contrast to the American Dream or Ethos of American middle-class society in 1960s and 1970s, Updike has depicted people in hopeless marital and social situations. Anxiety is the theme of 1960s and Updike is a chronicler of middle-class American anxiety. His characters treated with sympathy and simplicity, are often the tension of his characters' struggle to determine what is right, to know how to behave as changing individuals in a constantly changing world.

John Updike was born on March 18, 1932 in Reading Pennsylvania. Updike's family origins were strictly lower middle class. His father Wesley Russell Updike, was a high school Math teacher and his mother, Linda Grace Hoyer Updike, worked at Pomeroy's Department Store. She was a frustrated writer who actually began publishing stories late in life. In 1945 he and his family moved to a farmhouse originally owned by Hoyers in Plowville, a small village about ten miles south of Reading. Updike began his education in Shillington public school. His first publication was, *A Handshake with the Congressman*, which appeared in Shillington High school 'Chatterbox' in 1945. Updike was encouraged to write by his mother, who had the writing talent and saw the same in her son.

He graduates Shillington High school as senior class president & co-valedictorian in 1950. Updike's mother was particularly ambitious for her son. Having noted that Harvard had produced more than its fair share of authors, she became determined that John should go to Harvard. After an aunt gave eleven-year-old John a subscription to The New Yorker, he decided that his goal in life was to publish in that magazine, probably as a cartoonist.

In 1950 he entered Harvard, as he was given a full scholarship. His family could hardly have afforded otherwise. He graduated from Harvard summa cum laude (he wrote a thesis on Robert Herrick) in 1954 with a degree in English. In 1955, he joined The New Yorker staff writing editorials, poetry, stories and criticism. He became a "Talk of the town" writer for The New Yorker. He was offered a staff position at the magazine. He stayed in the New York only for two years and then moved to Ipswich, Massachusetts and devoted full time to writing. He died of lung cancer on 27 January 2009. Updike, an interpreter of American relationship, is only the third American who has received both the National Humanities Medal (2003) and the National medal of Arts (1989). He is also only the third American to win a second Pulitzer Prize in the fiction category. Updike is widely recognized for his careful craftsmanship and prolific output.

Updike's preoccupation with loss and social decay finds repeated expression throughout his oeuvre, most persuasively in the "Rabbit" novels, where cultural disintegration is most clearly associated with the breakdown of Christian religion. The four "Rabbit" novels collectively describe forty years of American history, and Rabbit's actions and reactions suggests a general view of the temper of the times as felt by an American Everyman.

Updike realistically portrayed the muddled, junk-food-guzzling patriotic small town American male and his failure in marriage and in life. In his "Rabbit" books – he created an engagingly flawed hero who somehow seemed to symbolize the American everyman: Harry "Rabbit" Angstrom, a former basketball champion turned second-hand car dealer trapped in a tedious marriage from which he seeks refuge in extra-marital affairs. Updike exhibits, a certain boldness in placing at the centre of a novel an average, unintellectual, politically conservative, working-class figure. Harry represents the confusions, anxieties, lack of spiritual concerns and blind longings of the middle class American of 1950s and 1960s.

In the first novel of the tetralogy, *Rabbit, Run*, the protagonist,

Harry "Rabbit" Angstrom, is a man in the middle, a middle-class father sandwiched between the competing demands of sensuality and society, the sacred and the profane. He is a common man who is sensual and prone to error. Rabbit, Run is a story of the angst of a young man who strives for the same perfection and skill in life that he had known on the basketball court. The novel begins with Rabbit married two years and working as a Magipeel kitchen demonstrator, returns to his cramped apartment to find his, pregnant wife Janice who drinks too much and watches children's program on T.V. and no longer attracts or responds to him much in bed. When Rabbit goes to fetch his two-year-old son Nelson from his mother's apartment, he sees his parents so enraptured by feeding his boy that he feels no longer needed by his family. Fed-up by his humiliating job and by his fear of becoming like his father he runs away from this second-rate life to reclaim his first-ratedness. He drives south toward the cotton fields, but after getting lost in West Virginia, he returns to Mt. Judge. Soon Rabbit is living with a part-time whore, Ruth, who also becomes pregnant, but he comes back home when he learns that his wife is in labor, leaving Ruth as abruptly and unthinkingly as he had left his wife. When he runs out again on Janice, she accidently drowns their baby. After the baby's funeral, he rejects the guilt others seem to be heaping on to him and takes off again, running for his life.

George J. Searles writes: "Harry's vacillation between hardheartedness and what Ruth terms his "mildness" is an adjunct of his entrapment in the snares of contemporary absurdity" (Roth and Updike 74). Updike appears to exonerate Harry by suggesting that his irresponsibility reflects a larger, national confusion. Harry's shortcomings are less guilty than they seem, Updike implies, because Harry's entire milieu is so compromised. Updike has created a character whose disaffiliation derives not only from that one character's anxieties, but from the failure of desacralized modern life to provide stable referents. Harry is as he is because –to a great extent— "external circumstances" have made him so:

the pathos of Rabbit Angstrom arises from the irredeemable waste of his alternate possibilities; and the significance of his story is the sobering point of view it provides on a civilization whose institutions and values are apparently disintegrating, a civilization losing the power to civilize... the ultimate loss is frighteningly more than just his own. (Burhans 350)

Updike wondered if in following his urge Rabbit would make the social fabric unravel, but Updike's knot of images suggests that the social fabric is far stronger than Rabbit and, in the end, entangles him. In a dream he realizes that his daughter is safely in God's hands, and Nelson as well, and that he must found a new religion. These images suggest that Rabbit's "inner strivings" are not separate from his own desire to keep the social order intact through comforting the ill and seeking divine help in the face of personal tragedy. Rabbit is no saint, but his inner strivings cannot be ignored. It seems doubtful, though, that running overcomes Rabbit's angst, for when we encounter him in the sequel, Rabbit Redux, Rabbit has returned home, and he has continued for ten years to resist the temptation of the gardens of inner striving. He even avoids the garden of sex not only in adultery but with his own wife. He has returned to society and supported his family, but the angst remains.

Rabbit has been seen as social rebel, wrongdoer, existential quester, anti-hero, saint and scoundrel. The central problem here is, is Rabbit immature in the sense of being irresponsible, selfish and damaging to others? Or is there a sense in which he stands for values of pre social innocence, instinct, even spiritual grace, are lost to social man? Rabbit, Run ignores political affairs to concentrate solely on an egotist trying to sustain his rebellion on the last debris of a vanishing national myth.

Rabbit Redux is a convincing sequel, largely because the Harry Angstrom portrayed in Rabbit, Run reappears here thoroughly a creature of his changed time, caught in its social crises, shaped by his class and surroundings as they have evolved into the late 1960's. *Rabbit Redux* is a curiously old-fashioned novel, dealing with

America's heightened consciousness of wrong-doing, at home in its oppressive treatment of black Americans, and abroad in its waging so futilely so brutal a war. Just over the horizon is America's bicentennial, and it is as if Updike is writing a spiritual and sociological history of the nation as it approaches its third century. Updike perhaps appropriately deals with the loss of the American dream. In this technologically fast progressing world money, materialism and facilities are increasing but happiness is shrinking. As Janice says 'I think our generation, the way we were raised, makes it hard for us to love life" (Rabbit Angstrom 329) and Peggy says, "Living is a compromise, between doing what you want and what other people want" (360).

In *Rabbit Redux*, Redux is Latin for 'brought back' Harry is middle aged bourgeois, who finds his life shattered by the infidelity of his wife. His wife Janice leaves him, she is having an affair, and we see the world at least initially from her point of view. The scene is the summer of 1969, the summer of the first moon landing and riots in the streets of American cities. After Janice takes off, he lives at home with his teenage son, then takes in an 18-year old runaway girl, Jill and a young black fugitive, Skeeter who has been to Vietnam and now dreams of becoming the black Jesus. Technology has changed his mother's life too. Old and ill, she is propped up and pepped up by a pill that brings her sexual fantasies she presumably never had as a healthy woman. Novel ends on a tragic note with the death of Jill in Rabbit's house and beginning of a never-ending hostility between Harry and his son, but the burning of the house is also indicative of a new beginning in Harry's life.

Updike places the thirty-six-year-old Rabbit in a precise social context linked to the recent years of relative affluence, deepening national malaise, and mass- produced inauthenticity. Rabbit Redux deals with post mythic lucidity, shows a concern with contemporary history which is all the more striking as Updike's involvement with America had been hitherto of a sentimental rather than a political nature. In this novel, for the first time in his career, Updike deals in a large way with public subjects: violence, the Vietnam war, black revolution, drug addiction, middle American anger and frustration, hippie life-styles, the moon shot. With great narrative facility he has integrated these volatile elements within a realistic novel of suburban life in 1969. "His real interest is the mystery of the human consciousness, that swarming riot of impressions, recollections, and impulses" (Searles Modern American Literature 308). Against a background of campus riots, student protest, New Left militancy, and war in Vietnam, the book pronounces, beyond any doubt, the death of the American Dream. The Rabbit books cover oil crisis and the scourge of Aids, becoming a chronicle of the disintegrating American dream.

Although the novel is rich in cultural details of 1960s yet Updike has again skilfully mingled them with the troubles of an American middleclass family man, a seeker, an anti-hero who is in search of some meaning and happiness in his life but despite the best of his efforts he is unable to find them. In the previous novel we blame it on Harry's running away from Janice. But in Rabbit Redux he has returned and is trying to be a responsible family man. But still things are badly messed up as he himself says, "I went to work days after days for ten years…I was a nursemaid to this machine but now they've retired the machine. I was nursemaid to Janice but she upped and left…Then I was nursemaid to Nelson and he hates me because I let Jill die" (587). After his house burned – down he asks his sister Mim, "What did I do wrong? I was a fucking good Samaritan. I took in these orphans. Black, white, I said Hop aboard. Regardless of color or creed…Free eats. I was the fucking Statue of Liberty…I did what felt right" (577). It is only at the end of the novel that there seems to be a sign of reconciliation, order and 'redux'.

In his novels Updike has portrayed the challenges given by the modern sensibilities. The traditional concept of family has been losing its importance. Everyone is busy thinking about his personal happiness and people have started taking family responsibilities as a burden or a duty that can be performed only by sacrificing one's own self. Family love and bond means nothing to modern people as if they are isolated from it.

In Updike's fictional world, family relationships are rendered all the more difficult by the fact that the persons involved exists in a period of shifting values and changing assumptions. Updike witnesses the degradation of his favourite locale with an acuteness of vision. Wherever he goes, Rabbit is confronted with the artificiality and cheap commercialization that have invested Brewer and its surroundings. "America has fallen from grace," and the pioneer's ethics can no longer provide the bewildered contemporaries with a meaningful standard of reference. There is a very perceptible blend of both affection for and dissatisfaction with the particular American ethos that Updike's works embody, reflect, and comment upon.

Conclusion: Common to all of Updike's works is a concern with individual moral responsibility and guilt, coupled with a clear-cut indictment of current values and a quixotic yearning to recapture the simpler and presumable purer American past. In this regard we could say that Updike as a social realist has closely observed the social changes of his times. The social, political, economic and cultural milieu of the 1960s was mirrored in his novels. The decade is known for political divisions, disruptions, and uncertainties in which writers came to terms with changing attitudes toward social involvement, government and corporate power, individual and minority rights, drug use, and technological advances like television and consumer air travel. His fiction disintegrated the American Dream of a happy nuclear family which was depicted and marketed by the media of that time. A consciously religious writer, he repeatedly creates confused, unfulfilled characters unable to reconcile the opposed demands of the self and the social contract, particularly in thc context of interpersonal relationships. Parents and children, husband and wives, lovers and friends encounter difficulties because they cannot strike a balance between personal happiness and social, moral obligations. Usually this failure is linked to sexual greed, and the resulting dilemmas are played out against a depressing background of vulgar materialism. Updike's novels convincingly portray his overriding theme of cultural disintegration, and disillusionment of American dream.

Works Cited:

"American Dream." Wikipedia the Free Encyclopedia. Wikipedia Foundation. 10 June 2013. <en.wikipedia.org/wiki/American_Dream>

Aristotle. Poetics. Wikipedia the Free Encyclopedia. Wikipedia Foundation. 5 June 2013.

<http://en.wikipedia.org/wiki/Poetics_(Aristotle)>

Boswell, Marshall. John Updike's Rabbit Tetralogy: Mastered Irony in Motion. Missouri: University of Missouri Press, 2001.

Burhans, Clinton S., Jr. "Things Falling Apart: Structure and Theme in Rabbit, Run." Studies in the Novel 5.3 (1974): 350.

"Ethos" Wikipedia the Free Encyclopedia. Wikipedia Foundation. 10 June 2013.<en.wikipedia.org/wiki/Ethos>

Friedan, Betty. Feminine Mystique. New York: W.W. Norton and Co., 1963.<http://nationalhumanitiescenter.org/ows/seminars/tcentury/FeminineMystique.pdf> Gingher, Robert S. "Has John Updike Anything to Say?" Modern Fiction Studies. 1974.

Excerpt in Contemporary Literary Criticism. Ed. Carolyn Riley and Phyllis Carmel Mendelson.Vol. 5. Detroit: Gale Research, 1976.

Howard, Jane. "Can a Nice Novelist Finish First?." Life 4 November 1966.<http://books.google.co.in/books?id>

Kluger, Richard. New York Herald Tribune Book Section. 7 April 1963. Excerpt in Modern American Literature. Ed. Mike Tyrkus. 5th ed. St James Press, 1998.

Markle, Joyce B. Fighters and Lovers: Theme in the Novels of John Updike. New York: New York

Univ. Press, 1973.

Rhode, Eric. "An Interview with Updike." Picked-Up Pieces. Ed. John Updike. New York: Knopf, 1975.

—. "Grabbing Dilemmas: John Updike Talks about God, Love and the American Identity." Vogue, 1 February 1971.

Samuels, Charles Thomas. "The Art of Fiction XLIII: John Updike." Paris Review, Winter 1968.<http://www.theparisreview.org/interviews/

4219/the-art-of-fiction-no-43-john-updike>. Searles, George J. The Fiction of Philip Roth and John Updike. Carbondale: Southern Illinois
University Press, 1985.
Updike, John. Rabbit Angstrom: A Tetralogy. New York: Everyman's Library – Knopf, 1995.

4. Objects and Bodies in José Saramago's '*Things*': A Postmodern Thing Theory Perspective

Mandeep Kaur

Abstract: The paper seeks to analyse the short story 'Things' which is part of a collection of short stories Lives of Things written by José Saramago. The analysis is approached through the perspective of the thing theory given by Bill Brown. Thing theory is about the ponderance on objects as things that exist in relation to interaction with human subjects. The narrative is centred around things and is driven by things than character or plot. Things construct meaning and shape the life around us. The paper aims to touch on the themes of isolation in contemporary urban life, the construction of identity, the meaning of things and the political undertones and circumstances during which the story was written. The paper studies the style and symbolicism prevalent throughout the story. As things are at the forefront, they facilitate their relationship with humans by means of asserting themselves resulting in a changed relationship with human subjects their conspicuous absence creates unfamiliarity and thus they shed their socially encoded value and herald a make new meaning for human life. Things are used to materialise religion, political convictions and ideology. Things deliver a political message and bring it into the consciousness of human beings, thus puts forward a change in the previous running perspective. Things metamorphosise into human bodies commenting on the bodies being treated as things. The consciousness alters to surface a new meaning for humans.

Keywords: Thing, Thing theory, Objects, and Government.

The term thing theory was coined in 2001 by Bill Brown. Although it was Martin Heidegger "may be regarded as the father of thing theory" (Pagan 1). Heidegger's work on things stresses the importance of the "thingness of the thing, to come out and reveal itself" (2). Literature makes the ordinary extraordinary, and defamiliarizes the familiar. Pagan states, "Readers are attracted to narratives not just because these narratives are character driven or plot driven but also because they are thing driven" (1). There are many works of art that enable us to see things from a perspective that we might not have otherwise. As Bill Brown notes in his essay on 'Thing Theory' about a novel 'Biographer's Tale' by AS Byatt- "fed up with Lacan as with deconstruction of wolf man, a doctoral student looks up at a filthy window..." (1). Here the object of attention is not the world that a window enables us to see but the window itself. We see things only by the virtue of what they are capable of giving to us not by what they themselves are. Things are defined solely on the basis of functions they perform to ease our lives. Their existence and utility depend on us. As Leo Stein puts it, "Things are what we encounter and ideas are what we project" (qtd in Brown 3) and also Brown observes, "We look through objects to see what they disclose about history, society, nature or culture- above all what they disclose about us" (4). Even the word thing itself is used to sometimes fill in gaps owing to our missing words for other things. "Thing is a word that tends to index a certain limit... between nameable and unnameable, the figurable and configurable, the identifiable and unidentifiable: Dr Seuss, Thing one and thing two" (Brown 4,5).

Shklovsky in 'Art as Technique' says, "...art exists that one may recover the sensation of life; it exists to make one feel things, to make the stone stony [...] The technique of art is to make objects 'unfamiliar' [...] to increase the difficulty and length of perception because the process of perception is an aesthetic end in itself and must be prolonged." Shklovsky talks about the 'stoniness of stone which is precisely Heidegger's 'thingness of thing', to see and perceive objects as if you are seeing them for the first time. Pagan states, "Indeed, Heidegger believes that although science may tell us plenty about the physical properties of things, it can tell us nothing at all about "the thing as thing" .... All give priority not so much to what you bring to the literary text, but rather to what the text does to you" (30). Another feature that Pagan observes in Heidegger's work on thing is "Things can only take on the nature of "thingness" as a result of human interaction with them" (31).

Based on the above observations from the works on thing theory, I analyse a short story 'Things' published in a collection of short stories Lives of Things by José Saramago in 1978. Although, the English-translated text by Giovanni Pontiero was published in 2012.

José Saramago was a Portuguese writer and recipient of the Noble Prize in Literature. He was a proponent of liberal communism and because he was an atheist, he challenged the beliefs of God in his work The Gospel According to Jesus Christ which was censored by the then government who claimed it to be religiously offensive. "Saramago sets whimsical parables against realistic historical backgrounds in order to comment ironically on human foibles" ("José Saramago", Britannica). Some of his prominent works are - Blindness, All the Names and Death with Interruptions etc.

Saramago belonged to peasant background but he worked as a technical mechanic and did some other odd jobs, it was during this time that he was inclined to read literature in public libraries and it was when he lost his job as a deputy director of some newspaper due to political reasons and he was unable to find further employment that he decided to fully devote himself to writing works of literature and this also shaped his political opinions. Lives of Things is one of the works of his early period as a writer. This was also the time period that followed the corporate authoritarian dictatorship of Antonio Salazar in Portugal. Saramago's work as a whole is often evaluated in the light of his liberal communist ideals. His works were often coloured with the influence of his political convictions and his views against religious orthodoxy. Lives of Things, in particular, was largely a response to Salazar's authoritarian government which was overthrown in 1974, after the Carnation Revolution.

Saramago wrote political allegories that's why oftentimes he is compared to George Orwell. Apart from this, he opted for an experimental style. He used long sentences sometimes as long as up to two pages separated by commas instead of full stops. He chose a loose flow of clauses. He did not delimit the dialogues of characters with quotation marks but rather capitalise the first letter of the speaker's dialogue to mark differences from other dialogues.

In the short story Things, he addresses serious matters with empathy for the human condition and isolation of contemporary urban life. His characters struggle with their need to connect with one another, form relations and bond as a community, and also with their need for individuality and to find meaning and dignity outside of political and economic structures.

In the story, the things on which humans rely start rebelling against their exploitation by simply disappearing. It starts with the sofa being too warm to sit on and proceeds to the disappearance of whole apartment buildings leading to the death of their inhabitants. Humans start to fight back with an attack on the part of the city, only to find out that they are rebelling using those very things including- bombs cannons, and copters against things. The irony is that, as soon as they prepare to attack things using other things, they disappear both on which the attack is to be done and through which the attack is to be done. The whole city vanishes leaving an empty space behind and people who are gathered to watch this phenomenon, to relish the revenge, and their clothes also vanish. Now, they are standing naked. At the end of the story, it is found that those disappeared things are living in the wild and metamorphosised into humans, commenting, "Never again will people be treated as things."

The story's protagonist is simply called a civil servant throughout the story. Even other characters, that he comes in contact with, are not named. This approach of not naming characters "Could this be part of the process of dehumanizing the subject?" as Pagan observes, "Could this indicate a subject whose dying coincides with the coming to life of an object – a thing, one of the things of the title?" (37). It even questions the construct of identity as to what constructs identity, as far as the story is concerned identity remains a political construct. The characters' social status is decided by a green letter etched on their hands. A civil servant has the letter 'H' engraved on his hand. The letters are decided by the government. Various letters such as A, B, C etc decide the social stature of people. Such as category C is classified as a lower category and some other categories such as A enjoy more privileges provided by the government. It is in the hands of the state to promote its status and decide the standard of living of its people. "Category H (he opened his right hand and saw the green letter) he would have to save for ages before he could afford the carpet, he had dreamed all these years" (Saramago). It shows how in order to get certain things to improve living they have to work towards being the pet of their government.

"He walked down the street, keeping a watchful eye on everything, inanimate or mobile, looking out for any suspicious behaviour as the Government (G) requested. He noticed others doing exactly the same and he found this demonstration of civic awareness reassuring although each and every one of them, in a manner of speaking, was competing for category C. 'There will be room for everyone,' he thought to himself" (Saramago). An object becomes a thing when it stops working and thus comes to our notice. 'Civic Awareness', here, is not awareness but actually blindness, blindly following the rules as government requested, how even the humans ruled by the government are no less than mere things for them. Just as things are taken for granted so are humans. Brown says, "takes objects for granted only in order to grant them their potency-to show how they organize our private and public affection" (7).

As things are disappearing leaving a lot of spaces in city, Civil servant observes, "The population seems to have multiplied"; "There were no ruins, only a void", there was a war but a mute, silent one resulting in emptiness leaving humans agape wondering what went wrong. (Saramago)

Pagan in his analysis of the story says, " a plethora of objects jostle for main character's attention and trigger a wide variety of emotions" ranging from "...paranoia, fear, and hatred turning to wrath followed by enjoyment at the prospect of revenge" (38). As the government has organised "an aerial bombardment of considerable part of the city and Civil servant leaves the city and climbs a hill in order to get a better view of the destruction... without dropping a single bomb and the cannons and other weapons on the ground remain silent and even disappear" (38). Civil servant is killed by a naked man and woman, now so many of them emerge out of woods in the wild above hills. This act of civil servant climbing up the hill, above his fellowmen in order to get a better view of destruction runs parallel to his desire to rise and progress to better his social status. Things that are metamorphosised into humans, live naked without any mark on their hands defining their identity. Their living on hill symbolically renders them at a high stature than humans who are living below, in the city. And living in the wild, naked could be symbolic morally, a return to primitive self, beyond the corrupted influence of politics or blind faith in governments making humans fight for a better standard of living. As even Pagan reinstates- "Could it be that all of these naked people do not have letters in their palms and represent a new population that will not bow down to the yoke of oppression, blindly following orders handed down by the top echelons of society. The civil servant's mistake was to allow himself to be treated like a thing – blindly following the promptings of those in authority. He (and his kind?) have been vanquished in order for the society to be reborn. As a woman proclaims at the very end, "Never again will men [of course she means "men and women"] be treated as things" (39).

Saramago's short story breathed life into things. The story demonstrates- "how inanimate objects constitute human subjects, how they move, how they threaten them, how they facilitate their relation to other subjects" (Brown 7). What Micheal Taussig questions in relation to Sylvia Plath's last poems can be questioned in case of short story 'Things' too- "does death have the capacity both to turn people things and to bring inanimate objects to life" (qtd in Brown 7).

In the story, government's decision to destruct the city, declare a war can be looked in relation to acts by governments around the world, for instance- "Taliban obsessively obliterates figures of Buddha, does the state thinks it destroys what it destroys?" (Brown 7). Demolition of Mandir to build Masjid or vice versa- what does the state thinks it destroys? Faith or monument, which is a thing only or is it the ideas that are projected onto things which are aimed to destroyed, and even after destroying do ideas actually die by that way? Each society imposes itself on subject's senses through certain things. "The question is less about "what things are for a given society than about what claims on your attention and on your action are made on behalf of things... How does the effort to rethink things became an effort to reinstitute society?" (Brown 9,10).

Brown remarks, "... this politicization of things inverted into materialization of politics" (10). Things are used to materialise religion, political convictions or ideology. Latour notes, "Things do not exist without being full of people" (qtd. in Brown 12). In the story things have the power to wipe out an entire city and bring about a society's rebirth. Saramago himself worked as a civil servant one time and when speaking in an interview to The Guardian in 2006, he said "The painter paints, the musician makes music, the novelist writes novels. But I believe that we all have some influence, not because of the fact that one is an artist, but because we are citizens. As citizens, we all have an obligation to intervene and become involved, it's the citizen who changes things. I can't imagine myself outside any kind of social or political involvement" (Stephanie). He was against the blind faith imparted in governments, much evident as an undercurrent that runs in his stories, where he blatantly mocks the working of goverment and its dehumanization of its subjects. No doubt 'Things' was one such story, as a political allegory that mocked the authoritarian regime of Salazar and also the blind faith put by people in it. Things acted as mirrors to highlight the shortcomings of humans and revealed how human bodies are things too.

The story was quite postmodern, the way it fits in thing theory. As Brown notes - "Only belatedly, in the 1980s, did Baudrillard declare that just as modernity was the historical scene of the subject's emergence, so postmodernity is the scene of the object's preponderance" (14).

The story holds a certain timelessness in it, for even now the government has made an identity- Aadhaar card, for each one of us to know our whereabouts whenever and however it pleases, and also how we are tied to a thing to know and get to other things.

Conclusion: Things act as mirrors to the ideas, values, fetishes, totems that are attached to them or maybe they attach themselves to and those ideas and values construct our everyday world view. Things shape meaning for us, the materiality constructs and constricts the cultural or political consciousness around us and transforming a way to view them, transforms the social world view. In the story, things brought a political consciousness to human beings and led to the transformation of their world. Nonetheless, things metamorphosise into bodies, to deliver the notion that as an agent of ideas they help bring conciousness about the corruption that is being done to human bodies, the things.

Works Cited:

"António de Oliveira Salazar." Wikipedia, Wikimedia Foundation.

https://en.m.wikipedia.org/wiki/Ant%C3%B3nio_de_Oliveira_Salazar. Accessed 10 June 2021.

"Big Think Interview with Bill Brown." Youtube, uploaded by Big Think, 24 Apr. 2012.

https://youtu.be/W41fUUbPnOw.

Brown Bill, "Thing Theory." Critical Inquiry, vol. 28, No. 1, Uni Chicago Press, 2001, 1-22.

"José Saramago." Britannica, www.britannica.com/topic/memoir-historical-genre. Accessed 17 June 2021.

"José Saramago." Wikipedia, Wikimedia Foundation, https://en.m.wikipedia.org/wiki/Jos%C3%A9_Saramago. Accessed 10 June 2021.

Meritt, Stephanie. "Interview: Still a street-fighting man". The Guardian, 30 Apr. 2006.

www.google.com/amp/s/amp.theguardian.com/books/2006/apr/30/fiction.features1. Accessed 3 June 2021.

Pagan, Nicholas A. "Thing Theory and the Appeal of Literature." Dacoromania litteraria 2.1

(2015): 28-42.

Saramago, José. The Lives of Things: Short Stories. Translated by Giovanni Pontiero London, Verso, 2013.

Shklovsky, Viktor, "Art as Technique" Russian Formalist Criticism: Four Essays, Edited by Lee T.

Lemon and Marion J. Reiss, Lincoln, University of Nebraska Press, 1965, 3-24.

5. Migration and Displacement: A Study of *Sea of Poppies* by Amitav Ghosh

Jaibhagwan

Abstract: Sea of Poppies, the first book of the Ibis trilogy, portrays a space where people from lower social classes face humiliation and exploitation publicly and individually. Therefore, when they get a chance to move away from their native land, they decide to leave. Although their circumstances compel them to leave, it is ultimately their decision. This type of Diaspora consists of both force and choice. The oppressed individuals are disappointed with their current life. The members of Ibis, including Deeti, Kalua, Paulette, Neel, Ah Fatt, and other passengers, share a common past of disrespect and filth, which unites them on the ship and allows them to create a new identity. On the ship, they find freedom and individuality as they transform and rebuild their identities. All passengers are migrants from different places, headed towards the same destination, Mareech Island. Deeti and Kalua conceal their true identities to live a new life amidst rapidly changing situations and locations, ultimately gaining a more authentic and respected identity.

Keywords: Diaspora, Identity, Migration.

Post-colonial literature deals with the consequences and issues of European colonization, focusing on the impact of colonialism on cultures and societies. It explores the conflicts between rulers and subjects, mainstream and marginalized groups, and oppressors and oppressed individuals. Colonized people were forced to accept their inferiority to their colonizers, resulting in clashes between personal and cultural identities due to disrespect and disregard for native values and culture. By applying theories of post-colonial theorists like Homi Bhaba, Gayatri Chakravorthy Spivak, and Edward W. Said, this field of study highlights the history of oppression in colonial and post-colonial societies.

Ann Loomba defines colonialism, "as the conquest and control of other people's land and goods" that resulted in "a wide range of practices including trade, plunder, negotiation, warfare, genocide, enslavement and rebellion" (2). Elleke Boehmer defines colonialism as "the settlement of territory, the exploitation of resources, and attempts to govern the indigenous inhabitants of occupied lands" (2). Post-colonialism is a literary theory concerned with the impact of colonialism on the culture and thinking of the colonized population. Mc Leod defines post colonialism as "a mode of reading texts concerned with the workings and legacy of colonialism either in the past or the present" (33). It examines the legacy of colonialism both in the past and present. In cultural studies, the term post-colonialism is applied not only to the formal end of colonialism but also to the historical process initiated by European aggression, beginning with the infiltration of British traders into Indian society through the British Raj. Post-colonialism covers all the cultural works affected by the imperial process from the moment of colonization to the present day, indicating a continuity of preoccupation throughout history. Ashcroft et al. Use the term 'post-colonial' "to cover all the culture affected by the imperial process from the moment of colonization to the present day... because there is a continuity of preoccupation throughout the historical process initiated by European aggression" (2).

The field of study involves various issues such as ambivalence, diaspora, hybridity, the quest for identity, ethnicity, and subalternity. Ambivalence is the unclear perception that the oppressor and the oppressed have towards each other, where the colonizer considers the colonized inferior, and the colonized view the colonizers as corrupt. Diaspora refers to the forced or voluntary displacement of people from their homelands, leading to a sense of rootlessness, identity crisis, and the search for identity. Hybridity is the creation of new cultural forms resulting from cross-cultural exchanges, whether social, political, linguistic, or religious. Subaltern refers to the colonized classes that have limited access or no access to cultural imperialism.

The novel *Sea of Poppies* by Amitav Ghosh delves into the opium trade of the 1830s that inflicted addiction on the Chinese population. It is the first instalment of the Ibis trilogy, named after a ship that was used for carrying slaves. The ship was purchased by an English company owner with the intention of shipping opium to China. However, due to the dispute over the opium trade, the ship is diverted to carry indentured slaves to sugar plantations in Mauritius. During the British rule in India, prisoners who were considered criminals, including dacoits, rebels and hooligans, were sent to island prisons such as Penang, Bencoolen, Port Blair and Mauritius as a form of punishment. Regarding to the plot, Dr B.K. Nagarajan said in his article Deconstruction Human Society: An Appreciation of Amitav Ghosh's *Sea of Poppies*,

Sea of Poppies tells the story of how it is that in the ship Ibis, headed to Caribbean sugar plantations; small new worlds are forged, bringing together north Indian women, Bengali Zamindars, black man, rural laborers and Chinese seamen. It is a story of people whose fate is written by poppy flower, the British who forced opium cultivation on farmers, the ruined lives of farmers, the people who were addicted and poor factory workers, deceit of the British, ship that transported the opium and which carried Indians to life of slavery. (102-103)

Amitav Ghosh's *Sea of Poppies* is a powerful narrative that explores themes of colonialism, postcolonialism, and migration, portraying a transnational diaspora that forms a collective identity, shedding its inessential ethos and milieus. The novel highlights the plight of the Indian people during the early nineteenth century, as they sought new routes towards a brighter future, leaving behind their historical roots. The story opens with the protagonist Deeti's visions of the Ibis ship and opium poppies, symbolizing the colonial history of the East. The novel depicts life in mid-nineteenth century India and its rural hinterland, as well as the passengers' lives on the Ibis, a ship that was previously used to transport slaves but has been remodelled for the new transport. The story is told in a modified language of the period, combining British and Indian English, ships lore, pirate talk, pidgin, and other verbal music of the Indian Ocean and Arabian Sea. Satwana Halder is in the view that, "the sea forms the background of the novel and the ship the Ibis, which had earlier been used for transporting slaves and was now remodelled for, the new transport, is at the centre" (342).

Sea of Poppies is a novel that explores the devastating impact of British colonialism and its policies on human lives. The story is set on the brink of the Opium Wars and follows a diverse cast of characters on a life-changing journey. It starts with Deeti, a wife and mother from a small Indian village who has a vision of a tall ship despite never having seen one before. The novel then shifts its focus to the Ibis, a merchant ship, and its crew, including Zachary Reid, a free mulatto from Baltimore who becomes the second-in-command of the Ibis with the support of the lascars. The ship travels around Africa to Mauritius and India to take aboard migrant workers, and Zachary meets Mr. Burnham, a British merchant who introduces him to the Anglo-Indian society. Burnham's agent, Baboo Nob Kissin, purchases the vessel and joins the voyage. Meanwhile, Deeti's husband dies, and she escapes death by sati with the help of Kalau, a local cart driver. They marry and join the workers headed abroad to Mauritius, as the novel portrays the impact of colonialism on the lives of ordinary people. Deeti was filled with terror upon discovering that she and others would be transported to Mareech, an island far away and seemingly inaccessible like Lanka. Ghosh's use of phrases such as "taken away," "never to be seen again," and "vanished" conveys the sense that this place was one of no return. Through Deeti's thoughts, the reader is shown the terrible situation faced by these people. She tries to imagine what it would be like to be in their place and realize that they would never again see their loved ones, their home, or even the holy river Ganga. Instead, they would be forced to live on a wild and demon-infested island, struggling to survive for the rest of their lives. Ghosh's powerful language highlights the immense suffering and despair of these individuals.

The novel continues with the introduction of another Indian character named Neel Rattan Haldar, a wealthy landlord who is heavily in debt and has been sentenced to seven years of forced labour abroad. He joins a group of workers headed for Mauritius, where he meets a Chinese opium addict named Ah Fatt. On board the ship, there are also two childhood friends, Paulette Lambert and Jodu, who have come for different reasons. Paulette seeks to escape an unwanted marriage and find a new life, while Jodu is seeking employment. Deeti, who is pregnant with her second child, is shocked to discover that her former husband's uncle is working as a guard on the ship and is still searching for her and Kalau, her current husband. The journey is difficult, with the migrants enduring abuse from some of the guards and facing the usual hardships of life at sea. Violence breaks out when Jodu is beaten by the first mate over a misunderstanding involving a woman. Deeti is also assaulted by Bhyro Singh, her former husband's uncle, and when Kalau tries to intervene, he accidentally kills one of the guards. Jodu plans to flee the ship with some other migrants, while Kalau turns the tables on Bhyro Singh during a beating and kills him. This leads to a severe beating and attempted lynching of Kalau by the guards.

The Captain of the ship, along with Zachary and another officer, steps in to stop the guards from unlawfully executing Kalau. The guards eventually back down, and Kalau is imprisoned. Meanwhile, Paulette and Deeti plan Kalau's escape and Jodu's escape attempt. Paulette reveals to Zachary that she is on board and aware of his racial status, causing tension between them. Mr.

Crowle discovers Zachary's racial status and attempts to blackmail him, but Ah Fatt kills him in revenge for the abuses he has endured. Zachary emerges from the cabin to discover Serang Ali, Jodu, Neel, Ah Fatt, and Kalau on a small boat paddling away from the Ibis. Zachary returns to his cabin and finds Paulette, Baboo Nob Kissin, and Deeti.

The theme of displacement and journeys is central to the novel, with characters moving for various personal, economic, or colonial reasons. The author focuses on the first wave of the Indian diaspora, often overlooked in diasporic writings, and uses historical research to provide an accurate depiction of the indentured diaspora in 19th-century India. The characters' experiences and circumstances act as catalysts for their movement, and the novel explores their reasons for displacement and how they cope with it. Ghosh documents the political and socioeconomic factors that caused a large-scale indentured labour migration of underprivileged Indian peasants to the Mauritius islands. A worldwide Indian Diaspora was developed as a result of indentured immigration. The novel begins in Deeti's village where poppy fields surround her home. Despite some personal issues, her life is relatively stable, homogenous, and confined to her local surroundings. Deeti has limited knowledge about the world beyond her village, as reflected in her narrow perspective.

Deeti knew that the vision was not materially present in front of her - as for example, was the barge moored near the factory. She had never seen the sea, never left her district, never spoken any language but her native Bhojpuri, yet not for a moment did she doubt that the ship existed somewhere and was heading in her direction. The knowledge of this terrified her, for she had never set eyes on anything that remotely resembled this apparition, and had no idea of what it might portend. (8)

The Ibis ship, which is a significant part of the novel, is portrayed in Deeti's vision. The ship's journey reveals that life on board is vastly different from the stable and localized world of Deeti's village. She comes from a world that is relatively uniform, while the crew of the Ibis, consisting of lascars, is incredibly diverse. Zachary discovers this as the story progresses. He had assumed they were a tribe or country, similar to the Cherokee or Sioux, but he now realised they were a diverse group of people who came from different parts of the world and shared only the Indian Ocean. They included Chinese and East Africans, Arabs and Malays, Bengalis and Goans, Tamils and Arakanese, as well as Arabs and Malays. Ghosh presents a new definition of migration by exploring the experiences of indentured laborers. His characters undergo physical translation and embark on a journey that holds significant meaning in the story. The journey across the Black Water, or Kala-Pani, is a symbol of overcoming fear and starting anew. It's important to note that in Indian culture, the ocean is typically viewed as a place of danger. Ghosh's language vividly captures the mental anguish of the people forced to leave their homeland. The experience is likened to being uprooted and torn away from their native soil. The author questions why fate would choose individuals who were deeply entrenched in their cultural roots and living far inland, rather than those who lived on the bustling coastlines. The people torn away from their homes were like a piece of the land's living flesh that fate had thrust its fist through, to tear away a piece of its stricken heart. Ghosh's language effectively conveys the pain and trauma experienced by these individuals.

The characters in *Sea of Poppies* represent a broad and cosmopolitan world by hailing from a range of ethnicities, linguistic backgrounds, religious affiliations, and cultural practises. The Ibis, the ship that serves as the book's focal point, is a meeting place for people from many backgrounds. While the protagonists try to establish a new life while hiding their true identities, their dislocation causes them to experience a new feeling of belonging. It portrays a diverse and multicultural world through the characters .The Ibis, the ship that is central to the novel, is a place where people from different walks of life come together. The characters' displacement triggers a new sense of belonging as they hide their actual identities and seek to start a new life. Deeti and Kalua, for example, change their names to adopt new identities. The novel explores the idea of race through the lens of displacement, diversity and multiculturalism. Deeti changed her name:

It was on her lips to identify herself as Kabutari-ki-ma, the name by which she had been known ever since her daughter's birth... her proper, given name was the first to come to mind and since it had never been used by anyone, it was as good as any. Aditi, she said softly, I am Aditi. (233).

The characters in the story are marginalized due to exploitation, migration, and colonialism. They are outsiders who are trying to move from the edges to the centre. For instance, Paulette, who is an orphan, disguises herself as a man to board the ship. Zachary Reid pretends to be white, while Deeti changes her name and runs away from her husband's funeral pyre along with her daughter.

Works Cited:

Ashcroft, Bill, Gareth Griffiths, and Helen Tiffin. The Empire Writes Back. Taylor's & Francis, 2004.

Boehmer, Elleke. Colonial and Postcolonial Literature: Migrant Metaphors. Oxford University Press, 1995.

Ghosh, Amitav. 2009. Sea of Poppies. New Delhi: Penguin.

Haldar, Satwana, "Exposing the Ugly Face of Colonialism: A study of Sea of Poppies." The Novels of Amitav Ghosh. Ed. R. K. Dhawan, Prestige Books, 2010,pp. 339- 52.

Loomba, Ania. Colonialism/Postcolonialism. Routledge, 1998.

McLeod, John. Beginning Postcolonialism. Manchester University Press, 2010.

Nagarjun Dr, B.K. Amitav Ghosh: A Critical Study. Omega Publishers, 2011.

6. Reconstruction of 'Image' of Women: A Study of Society's Perception of Beauty

Jasleen Kaur

"Women are somehow more biological, more corporeal, and more natural than men" (Grosz).

Abstract: For ages, the female bodies have been regarded as the products to be adorned and kept up to empower them to allure men into marriage so they would have the material way to live. Women regard for their bodies accordingly appeared as exhibiting them as commodities for society's evaluation. With the publication of *The Second Sex* by Simone de Beauvoir, feminist thinkers started talking about the relation between the body and the self. She was the first to talk about the sex/gender dichotomy in her work. Sex is a biological trait whereas the gender is a complete social construct. One of the major ideas of De Beauvoir's theory was that there is no 'essence' of a woman, a woman is constructed as such by men and the society she lives in. "One is not born a woman but becomes one" (Beauvoir).De Beauvoir was of the opinion that the role of women is conditioned by the society. She is trained and prescribed so as to assume the role of 'women' (Nayar 89). She recognised that 'to be present in the world implies strictly that there exists a body which is at once a material thing in the world and a point of view towards the world'(Beauvoir). The body, however, constitutes the self. It is not separated from the self as such. The body is not simply what biology introduced us to. It is also a body which is experienced by others whose reaction to it intervenes our own feeling of being.

Introduction: The reaction a body receives from society is different for both men and women, opines Beauvoir. It is the intertwining of the material and cultural factors that forms our identity. The way in which a young girl and a woman experiences her body is, for Beauvoir, a result of a process of internalising the view of it under the gaze of others. "Through compliments and admonishments, through images and words, she discovers the meaning of the words pretty and ugly; she soon knows that to be pleased is to be pretty as a pic- ture; she tries to resemble an image, she disguises herself, she looks at herself in the mirror, she compares herself to princesses and fairies from tales" (Beauvoir).

It is here, that the women commodify their bodies, as something to be gazed on. This is some- thing which has nothing to do with the anatomy of a body as such but with the society. Women start living their bodies in a particularly externalised way, disguising the look and delivering their bodies as something for other people.

The advent of social media, however, fuelled the making of the image of woman into being more conscious and insecure. Something is always too big, too small, too thin, too fat, too short or too long. Hours spent on mobile phones fuel mutual comparisons and evaluations. Young women tend to focus a lot on what they are not or do not have and they feel inadequate. We can- not escape the power of images. Pressure on women is also higher because the female body has been central to formation of women's identity for centuries. Isn't it the patriarchal society that at- tributes particular values to woman's body? Beauty contests commodify the women's body for the male gaze. Thinness associated with feminine beauty (seen in advertisements, films) drives young girls to drastic measures to lose weight. The woman's body, therefore, is only the object of study, control, discipline and gaze. The woman is never her own subject. Her body or the whole identity is determined by the societal norms and the beauty standards that are created by the society itself. Butler argued that far from being a set of fixed and stable values and role imposed by society, gender was a 'performance' or 'role' enacted by individuals. It is social in the sense that is validated by society. So, are women constantly performing to fit in the standards of beauty set up society? As Butler puts it, 'Identity is performatively constituted by the very "expressions" that are said to be its results.' The expressions are the discourses and representations.

When real women compare themselves with these norms of beauty most of them fall short. And think they are not beautiful enough or not thin enough or not toned enough! It is no longer a choice but an order to follow. Hours spent on scrolling down the news feed pages of these social media platforms fuel mutual comparisons and evaluation. Young women tend to focus a lot on what they are not or do not have and feel inadequate about their bodies. It is said that 'bikini was made to fit into the bodies, not the bodies were made to fit the bikini.'

The problem of the "ubiquity" of the bodily images is explored by feminist theorists such as Susan Bordo. For Bordo there is a link between the visual culture and the burden of weight for women. The way in which the perfected bodies have become normalised can be seen through number of images and their circulation on social media."These images are teaching us how to see. Filtered, smoothed, polished, softened, re- arranged. And passing. Digital creations, visual cyborgs, teaching us what to expect from flesh and blood. Training our perception in what's a defect and what is normal" (Bordo).

In this sense we are blurring the boundaries between our real self and virtual being. Magazines, the social media, films, advertisements and the fashion industry depicts the "impossible images" of women's body and this causes women to feel depressed about their own bodies and tell them that are not a proper fit for the society. Women in commercials are doomed to flawlessness and are sold as sex objects. People use filters in their pictures, edit them, play with the original colours; destructing the whole idea of aura attached to it (Benjamin). "If a shoe does not fit you. You don't blame your feet. You just go to find one that does. So, when a dress does not fit. Why blames our body? You are not meant to 'fit into clothes.' Clothes are meant to fit onto you" (Storyseller comics).

In the preface to Bodies That Matter, Butler says, " What about the materiality of the body, Judy?...an effort...to recall me to a bodily life that could not be theorized away...for surely bod- ies live and eat; eat and sleep; feel pain and pleasure; endure illness and violence; and these facts...cannot be dismissed as mere construction."She replies to such questions by giving a brief account of materiality of the body in terms of a process of 'materialisation.' Here she refers to the model of construction of a female body with society constantly acting on it. She concurs with the position of Spivak, to whom she even quotes in her work :

> "If one thinks of the body as such, there is no possible outline of the body as such. There are thinking of the systematicity of the body, there are value codings of the body. The body, as such, cannot be thought, and I certainly cannot approach it." (Spivak).

To meet this media triggered gap between self-perception and genuine body billion dollar indus- try has sprang up globally. Magazines and advertisements are marketed to help women "look better" by providing them information and products that are supposed to make them look and feel good. In the entertainment industry women are objectified to an extreme level. Several females are shown, wearing practically nothing, hanging around one man who is portrayed as their 'one all and be all.' There is a complex dynamic that exists among power, ideology, language, and its practice within a context of its socio-cultural milieu that could be manifested in the form of 'do- ing gender' and 'performing gender.' It is said that gender is a social entity. It is the role played by an individual not by choice but in accordance with the societal norms. For example, being a woman demands certain behaviour out of her that is acceptable in society. Repeated over time, this behaviour would become 'me' - that means 'gender' does not feel like a performance, but the natural way of living or behaving. The social media in the same way provides a stereotyped 'im- age', an imposition which has to be internalised by 'women' and exhibit their beauty that suits to the popular and dominant perception of the larger community. Standards of beauty being set up today are almost unattainable for most women. Be it any era, ancient or the modern or the post- modern, women have been encouraged to reconstruct their image to suit to the society's perception of beauty.

Though, there was a time when natural beauty was more desirable, but it seems that we departed from that a long time ago. It is, now, the age of filters, the age of comparison, the age of judge- ment, the age of social media!

Works Cited:

Beauvoir, Simone De. The Second Sex. Vintage, 201

Bordo, Susan. Unbearable Weight. University of California Press, 2004. Butler, Judith. Bodies That Matter. Routledge, 2014.

Documentary. The Social Media Beauty Cult I DW Documentary. YouTube, 8 Aug. 2019, https:// www.youtube.com/ watch?v=5PBs7RqPTrI.

Grosz, Elizabeth. Volatile Bodies. Routledge, 1994.

Hansen, Miriam Bratu. "Benjamin's Aura." Critical Inquiry, vol. 34, no. 2, 2008, pp. 336–375.

JSTOR, www.jstor.org/stable/10.1086/529060. Accessed 15 June 2021.

Kathleen. "Feminist Perspectives on the Body (Stanford Encyclopaedia of Philosophy)." Stanford Encyclopedia of Philosophy, https:// plato.stanford.edu/entries/feminist-body/#Bib. Ac cessed 15 June 2021.

Nayar. Contemporary Literary and Cultural Theory: From Structuralism To Ecocriticism. Pear son Education India, 2010.

7. Queer Theory and Feminism: Intersectionality and the Politics of Identity

Gulshan Kumar

Abstract: This paper explores the intersectionality of queer theory and feminism, and how both fields of the study challenge dominant power structures that perpetuate inequality and oppression based on gender, sexuality, race, class, and other social identities as outlined by Dore Bowen "while feminism is aligned with lesbian and gay politics in seeking liberation from oppressions based on gender and sexual identity, queer theory challenges the norms that constitute these identities" (145). Going beyond gender and sexuality, queer politics also advocates for "all kinds of economic, political, epistemological and cultural experiments that seek to produce difference and equality at the same time" (Lorenz 17). The concept of intersectionality is examined, which recognizes the interconnectedness of various social identities and how they shape experiences of oppression and privilege. The politics of identity is also discussed, with a focus on the ways in which individuals and groups are categorized and labeled based on their social identities. Queer theory and feminism both critique the dominant narratives and seek to empower marginalized individuals and groups by disrupting the politics of identity. Ultimately, this paper argues that through their shared commitment to intersectionality, queer theory and feminism contribute to creating a more just and equitable society.

Keywords: queer theory, feminism, intersectionality, politics of identity, power structures, oppression, privilege, social identities, marginalization, empowerment, dominant narratives, just and equitable society.

INTRODUCTION: -

Queer theory and feminism are two distinct yet interconnected fields of study that have emerged as responses to the marginalization and oppression of individuals based on their gender, sexuality, race, class, and other social identities. The queer theory emerged in the late 1980s and early 1990s as a response to the limitations of traditional gay and lesbian politics. Queer theory seeks to challenge dominant cultural norms and structures that perpetuate the marginalization of LGBTQ+ individuals. It also seeks to challenge the idea of fixed sexual and gender identities and instead posits that these identities are fluid and socially constructed. "The queer theory looks at the history of cultural representations of the gay/lesbian as deviant, sick, or criminal while foregrounding sexuality as an important category of critical analysis when dealing with cultural texts. Queer theory moves between literary analysis and activism because it shows how cultural representations contribute to very real material oppression of homosexuals" (Nayar 184).

The queer theory draws on a range of disciplines, including sociology, anthropology, and philosophy, to explore the complexities of gender and sexuality. Some of the key concepts in queer theory include:

Heteronormativity: the assumption that heterosexuality is the norm and that other forms of sexuality are deviant or abnormal.

Binary gender: the idea that there are only two genders, male and female, and that these genders are fixed and biologically determined.

Performativity: the idea that gender and sexuality are not innate but are instead constructed through performance and repetition.

Intersectionality: the recognition that gender and sexuality intersect with other forms of oppression, such as race and class, to shape individuals' experiences and identities.

While the queer theory has primarily focused on challenging the heteronormative assumptions and structures that dominate society and academia, feminism has sought to challenge patriarchal power structures that limit women's social, economic, and political agency. Feminism is a broad and diverse movement that has its roots in the late 19th and early 20th centuries. The movement seeks to challenge patriarchal structures and cultural norms that perpetuate gender inequality and limit women's opportunities and experiences. "The feminist theory tries to locate the basis for the woman as a subject of her own self, desires, and identity rather than as an object for the male. Subjectivity has been variously located by feminists in the body, collectivity, and the social" (Nayar 101). Feminism draws on a range of disciplines, including philosophy, sociology, and political science, to explore the complexities of gender and power. Some of the key concepts in feminism include:

Patriarchy: a social system in which men hold primary power and authority.

Gender inequality: the systematic disadvantage of women relative to men.

Intersectionality: the recognition that gender inequality intersects with other forms of oppression, such as race and class, to shape individuals' experiences and identities.

Essentialism: the idea that there are innate and essential differences between men and women that determine their respective roles and capabilities.

The personal is political: the idea that personal experiences of oppression and inequality are rooted in broader political and social structures.

However, both fields share a commitment to intersectionality and the politics of identity. They recognize the interconnectedness of various social identities and how they shape experiences of oppression and privilege. Through their critiques of dominant narratives, queer theory, and feminism aim to empower marginalized individuals and groups and create a more just and equitable society.

Intersectionality in understanding the politics of identity

Intersectionality is a concept that recognizes the complex and overlapping ways in which different forms of oppression, discrimination, and privilege interact and intersect within individuals' lives. It was originally developed within black feminist theory, but has since been applied more broadly to understand the experiences of individuals who face multiple forms of marginalization based on their race, gender, sexuality, class, and other aspects of their identity. "History verifies that black women have rejected doormat status, whether racially or sexually imposed, for centuries" (May 23).

The significance of intersectionality in understanding the politics of identity lies in its recognition that those individuals' experiences and identities are not singular or homogenous, but rather are shaped by multiple intersecting factors. For example, a black lesbian woman may experience discrimination based on her race, gender, and sexuality, and these forms of discrimination may intersect and reinforce one another to create unique experiences of marginalization. Intersectionality is important because it allows us to recognize the diversity of experiences within marginalized communities, and to understand the ways in which different forms of oppression can interact and compound one another. By recognizing these intersections, we can develop more nuanced and inclusive understandings of identity and can work towards social justice and equality efforts that are responsive to the needs of all individuals.

In the context of queer theory and feminism, intersectionality is particularly significant because it highlights the importance of centering the experiences and perspectives of marginalized groups. By recognizing the ways in which different forms of oppression intersect and interact, we can develop more nuanced and inclusive theories and practices that are responsive to the needs of all individuals, particularly those who have historically been excluded or marginalized within these fields.

Historical and Cultural Context

Social and political movements that paved the way for queer theory and feminism.

Queer theory and feminism emerged in response to social and political movements that sought to challenge dominant norms and systems of oppression. Some of the key historical and cultural contexts that paved the way for these fields include:

Civil Rights Movement: The Civil Rights Movement was a major turning point in the history of the United States, and had far-reaching impacts on social justice movements around the world. The movement was led by black activists who organized protests, boycotts, and other forms of civil disobedience to challenge the racist laws and policies that were pervasive throughout the country. The Civil Rights Movement paved the way for later social justice movements by demonstrating the power of collective action and mobilization.

Second Wave Feminism: Second Wave Feminism emerged in the 1960s and 1970s as a response to the limitations of First Wave Feminism, which had largely focused on women's suffrage and legal rights. Second Wave Feminism was marked by a growing awareness of the ways in which gender intersects with other forms of oppression, such as race and class, and emphasized the importance of recognizing women's experiences as unique and diverse. The movement led to important gains in women's rights, including the legalization of abortion and greater access to education and employment opportunities.

Gay Liberation Movement: The Gay Liberation Movement emerged in the wake of the Stonewall riots of 1969, which were a series of protests by LGBTQ+ individuals against police brutality and discrimination. The movement sought to challenge the idea that homosexuality was a mental illness or a moral failing, and called for greater recognition and acceptance of LGBTQ+ identities. The movement also paved the way for later queer activism and scholarship, by highlighting the ways in which heteronormativity and homophobia shape social and political institutions.

Black Feminism: Black Feminism emerged in the 1970s as a response to the limitations of mainstream feminism, which largely excluded the experiences of women of color. Black Feminism emphasized the importance of recognizing the ways in which race, gender, and class intersect to create unique experiences of oppression, and called for more inclusive and intersectional feminism. The movement paved the way for later scholarship and activism focused on the intersectionality of social identities.

Postmodernism: Postmodernism emerged in the late 20th century as a response to the limitations of modernist thought, which emphasized universal truths and objective knowledge. Postmodernism challenged these ideas by emphasizing the importance of subjectivity and context and highlighting the ways in which language and culture shape our understanding of the world. Postmodernism paved the way for later critical theory, including queer theory, by encouraging scholars to explore the ways in which power operates within language and culture.

Queer theory and feminism emerged within a broader historical and cultural context of social and political movements that sought to challenge dominant norms and systems of oppression. These fields continue to evolve and expand in response to ongoing struggles for social justice and equality.

Critique of traditional approaches to gender and sexuality

Traditional approaches to gender and sexuality have been criticized by feminist and queer theorists for their narrow and limited views. Here are some of the key critiques of traditional approaches to gender and sexuality:

Binary thinking: Traditional approaches to gender and sexuality have tended to be based on binary thinking, which assumes that there are only two genders (male and female) and two sexual orientations (heterosexual and homosexual). This binary thinking excludes the experiences of people who identify as non-binary or genderqueer and those who experience sexual attraction to multiple genders.

Essentialism: Traditional approaches to gender and sexuality have also been criticized for their essentialism, which assumes that gender and sexuality are innate and fixed characteristics of individuals. This essentialist view ignores the ways in which gender and sexuality are shaped by social and cultural factors, and can change over time.

Heteronormativity: Traditional approaches to gender and sexuality have tended to be based on a heteronormative perspective, which assumes that heterosexuality is the norm and all other forms of sexuality are deviant or abnormal. This perspective reinforces social norms and expectations around gender and sexuality and can lead to discrimination and marginalization of LGBTQ+ individuals.

Lack of intersectionality: Traditional approaches to gender and sexuality have often ignored the ways in which gender and sexuality intersect with other aspects of identity, such as race, class, and ability. This lack of intersectionality can lead to a narrow and incomplete understanding of the experiences of marginalized groups.

Traditional approaches to gender and sexuality have been criticized for their narrow and limiting views, which exclude the experiences of many individuals and perpetuate systems of oppression. Feminist and queer theorists have sought to challenge these traditional approaches and develop new frameworks for understanding gender and sexuality that are more inclusive and intersectional. "This utopian notion of sexuality freed from heterosexual constructs, sexuality beyond "sex", failed to acknowledge the ways in which power relations continue to construct sexuality for women even within the terms of "liberated" sexuality for women even within the terms of "liberated" heterosexuality or lesbianism" (Butler 71).

Critique of heteronormativity

Heteronormativity is a concept that has been developed by feminist and queer theorists to critique the assumption that heterosexuality is the norm and all other forms of sexuality are deviant or abnormal. Heteronormativity is a pervasive social and cultural norm that shapes our understanding of gender and sexuality and can lead to discrimination and marginalization of LGBTQ+ individuals.

Cisgender privilege: Cisgender privilege refers to the advantages and benefits that individuals who identify with the gender they were assigned at birth (i.e. cisgender individuals) have over individuals who do not. Cisgender privilege is closely related to heteronormativity, as it reinforces the assumption that gender is binary and fixed, and marginalizes individuals who do not conform to these norms.

Homonormativity: Homonormativity is a concept that has been developed to critique the ways in which mainstream LGBTQ+ movements and culture have adopted heteronormative values and norms, such as monogamy, marriage, and the nuclear family. Homonormativity can reinforce the marginalization of LGBTQ+ individuals who do not conform to these norms and can limit the possibilities for radical social change.

The fluidity of sexual and gender identities

The fluidity of sexual and gender identities is a central concept in contemporary feminist and queer theory. It challenges the traditional binary understanding of gender and sexuality and emphasizes the variability and diversity of these identities. Here are some key ideas related to the fluidity of sexual and gender identities: Non-binary gender identities: Non-binary gender identities refer to identities that fall outside the traditional binary categories of male and female. Non-binary gender identities can include identities such as genderqueer, gender fluid, or gender. These identities challenge the assumption that gender is a fixed and binary category and highlight the diversity of gender expressions and experiences.

Sexual fluidity: Sexual fluidity refers to the variability and changeability of sexual attraction over time. Sexual fluidity challenges the assumption that sexual orientation is a fixed and innate characteristic of individuals and instead emphasizes the ways in which sexuality can be shaped by social and cultural factors. Sexual fluidity can also challenge the rigid categories of heterosexuality and homosexuality, and highlight the ways in which individuals can experience attraction to multiple genders.

Queer resistance: Queer resistance refers to the ways in which individuals and communities resist and challenge heteronormative norms and expectations. Queer resistance can involve the adoption of non-binary gender identities or the exploration of fluid sexual orientations. It can also involve the creation of alternative communities and social structures that challenge mainstream heteronormative values.

The concept of the fluidity of sexual and gender identities is essential for challenging the traditional binary understanding of gender and sexuality and emphasizing the diversity and complexity of these identities. It also offers possibilities for imagining alternative futures and more inclusive and just societies. Intersectionality is a framework for understanding power structures that emphasizes the ways in which social identities (such as race, gender, class, and sexuality) intersect and interact to create unique experiences of oppression and privilege. Intersectionality highlights the ways in which these identities are not experienced in isolation, but rather are interconnected and shape individuals' experiences of power and marginalization.

Multiple systems of oppression: Intersectionality recognizes that individuals experience multiple systems of oppression simultaneously. For example, a person who is both a woman and a person of color may experience discrimination based on both gender and race. These systems of oppression are not experienced in isolation, but rather interact and reinforce each other to create unique experiences of marginalization.

Power structures and privilege: Intersectionality emphasizes the ways in which power structures and privilege operate within and across social identities. For example, a white woman may experience privilege based on her race, while still experiencing marginalization based on her gender. Intersectionality highlights the ways in which individuals' experiences of privilege and marginalization are shaped by the intersection of multiple social identities.

Agency and resistance: Intersectionality also recognizes the ways in which individuals and communities resist and challenge systems of oppression. Intersectionality highlights the ways in which individuals and communities can use their multiple identities and experiences of marginalization to create alternative forms of resistance and social change.

Complexity and nuance: Intersectionality emphasizes the complexity and nuance of individuals' experiences of power and marginalization. It recognizes that individuals are not simply defined by one social identity or one system of oppression, but rather are shaped by the intersection of multiple identities and experiences.

Intersectionality is a powerful framework for understanding power structures and the ways in which social identities intersect and interact to shape individuals' experiences of oppression and privilege. It emphasizes the importance of recognizing the complexity and nuance of individuals' experiences, and the possibilities for agency and resistance within systems of oppression.

Implications for understanding the politics of identity.

The concept of identity has become increasingly important in contemporary politics, with social movements centered around identity-based issues such as race, gender, sexuality, and nationality. Understanding the politics of identity requires an understanding of intersectionality, as different social identities intersect and interact with each other in complex ways. One implication of intersectionality for the politics of identity is that it challenges simplistic notions of identity politics that prioritize one form of identity over others. For example, some critics of identity politics argue that it divides people based on narrow categories and perpetuates division rather than unity. However, intersectionality shows that people have multiple identities and that these identities interact with each other in complex ways, meaning that any effective politics of identity must take into account the diversity of experiences and perspectives within marginalized communities.

Another implication of intersectionality for the politics of identity is that it highlights the importance of recognizing privilege and power within marginalized communities. Intersectionality shows that some identities are more privileged than others and that these power dynamics can play out within marginalized communities themselves. For example, a cisgender gay man may have more privilege than a transgender woman of color within the LGBTQ+ community. Recognizing these power dynamics is crucial for building more inclusive and equitable movements for social justice. Intersectionality has important implications for understanding the politics of identity by challenging simplistic notions of identity politics and highlighting the importance of recognizing privilege and power dynamics within marginalized communities. By taking an intersectional approach, we can work towards building more inclusive and equitable movements for social justice that recognize the diversity of experiences and perspectives within marginalized communities.

Critiques of theoretical abstraction and lack of practical application

One of the critiques of intersectionality is that it can be too theoretical and abstract, without clear guidelines for practical application. Some critics argue that intersectionality lacks concrete policy recommendations or actionable solutions for addressing the complex and interconnected issues facing marginalized communities. Another critique is that intersectionality can be too focused on individual identities, without sufficient attention to broader structural factors such as capitalism, colonialism, and neoliberalism. Some argue that intersectionality can lead to a form of identity politics that is disconnected from broader social and economic issues.

Finally, some have criticized the language and terminology used in intersectionality theory, arguing that it can be inaccessible or exclusionary to those outside of academia or certain activist circles. This can limit the reach and impact of intersectionality as a concept and movement. These critiques and challenges highlight the need for intersectionality to continually evolve and adapt to changing social and political contexts. While the concept of intersectionality has been influential in highlighting the complexity of social identities and experiences of oppression, it is important to ensure that it remains grounded in practical applications and solutions and that it takes into account broader structural factors and the diverse experiences and perspectives of marginalized communities.

Critiques of lack of inclusivity

Another critique of intersectionality is that it can be limited in its inclusivity. While intersectionality aims to recognize the complexity and interconnectedness of social identities, it may still center on certain identities or experiences, such as those of cisgender, heterosexual, able-bodied, and middle-class women. This can result in the exclusion or marginalization of individuals or groups who do not fit into these narrow categories, such as trans and non-binary individuals, disabled individuals, and those from low-income or working-class backgrounds. Moreover, some have argued that intersectionality can perpetuate a hierarchy of oppression, with certain identities or experiences being privileged over others. For example, the experiences of women who are white, able-bodied, and middle-class may be prioritized over those of women who are Black, disabled, and working-class. This can result in the erasure or invisibility of certain identities and experiences within intersectional frameworks.

To address these critiques, intersectionality needs to be more inclusive and center the voices and experiences of those who have been historically marginalized or excluded. This means paying attention to the ways in which different forms of oppression intersect and interact with each other, and recognizing the diversity of experiences and perspectives within marginalized communities. It also means being open to critiques and feedback from those who feel excluded or marginalized within intersectional frameworks and working to address these issues in a proactive and meaningful way.

Ongoing challenges and potential for future developments

Despite its contributions to social justice movements, intersectionality still faces ongoing challenges and opportunities for future development. Some of the key challenges include:

Co-optation and co-modification: There is a risk of intersectionality being co-opted by institutions or individuals who use it to appear progressive or inclusive without making meaningful changes to their policies or practices.

Intersectionality fatigue: There is a risk that intersectionality becomes too complex or overwhelming, leading to a sense of fatigue or burnout among those who are trying to apply it in their activism or research.

Resistance and backlash: There is a risk of resistance and backlash from those who feel threatened by intersectionality, either because it challenges their privilege or because they see it as divisive or too focused on identity.

To address these challenges and advance the potential for future developments, some possible strategies include: Re-centering the voices and experiences of those who have been historically marginalized or excluded within intersectional frameworks. And emphasizing the importance of solidarity and coalition-building across different social movements and identities. Recognizing the role of intersectionality in shaping policy and practice, and advocating for more inclusive and equitable approaches in all spheres of life. Continuing to engage in critical reflection and dialogue around the limitations and challenges of intersectionality, while also recognizing its ongoing potential for social change.

Intersectionality remains a powerful tool for understanding and addressing the complex and interconnected issues facing marginalized communities. By addressing ongoing challenges and fostering opportunities for future development, we can work towards building a more inclusive and equitable society for all.

Conclusion

In conclusion, the ongoing relevance and importance of queer theory and feminism cannot be overstated. Both fields have made significant contributions to challenging systems of oppression and promoting social justice, and their continued evolution and intersection, as exemplified by intersectionality, highlights the importance of recognizing the complex and interconnected nature of social identities and experiences of oppression. However, in order to truly build a more just and equitable society, we must move towards a more inclusive and intersectional approach that centers on the voices and experiences of those who have been historically marginalized or excluded. This requires a commitment to ongoing reflection, action, and transformation of power structures, and an understanding of the ways in which different forms of oppression intersect and interact with each other.

It also requires recognition of the limitations and challenges of intersectionality, and a willingness to engage in critical reflection and dialogue around these issues. By actively seeking out and amplifying diverse voices and experiences, and working towards more inclusive and equitable policies and practices in all spheres of life, we can build a more powerful and inclusive movement for social justice.

Ultimately, this call for continued critical engagement and transformation of power structures is essential if we are to create a society that truly values and respects the diverse experiences and identities of all its members. Only by working together towards this shared goal can we hope to create a future that is truly just, equitable, and inclusive for all.

Works Cited:

Butler, J. Gender trouble: Feminism and the subversion of identity. Routledge (P),1990.

Bowen,Dore. ''On the site of her own exclusion: strategizing queer feminist art history'' Otherwise: Imagining Queer Feminist Art History, edited by Amelia

Jones and Erin Silver, Manchester University (P),2016.

May, Vivan. Rethinking Women's and Gender Studies.Harper Collins (P),2012.

Nayar, Pramod K. Contemporary Literary and Cultural Theory. Pearson (P),2017.

Lorenz, Renate. Queer Art: A Freak Theory.Piscatsway: Transaction (P),2012.

8. Politics of Gender in Poile Sengupta's *Mangalam*

Dushrath Gutt

Abstract: The Feminist Theatre aims at doing justice to the position of woman and focuses on how to makea woman free from the control of man's psyche in her projection in drama. In recent times, it has marked its presence felt in India as well, though with limited playwrights like Manjula Padmanabhan, Dina Mehta, Polie Sengupta, Tripurarai Sharma and a few others. Polie Sengupta remains one of the most vocal voices in raising issues related to women-body, soul and mind. Women in Indian society which is overwhelmingly patriarchal remains at the margins in all walks of life and is subjected to various sorts of wrongdoings, maltreatment and violence, even at the private of the places which were hitherto regarded their own domain. By projecting women at public spaces through her dramaturgy, Poile wants to give subtle message to the forces controlling the gender projecting process that women understand the designs of patriarchy and will question and resist the existing order with whatever arsenal they have at their disposal with regard to secure the rightful position in Indian society. Her play *Mangalam*, a typical social play, exposes the stratagem adopted by those having control over gender determining roles to keep woman under control and at margins. The play juxtaposing two generations-traditional and modern- in its two acts captures conflict of gender roles and gradually captures signs of resistance and protest against the existing patriarchal structure of gender appropriating designs. The present chapter dissects the moves made by those at the margins-woman- to come out of the shadow of patriarchy asks for re-structuring and redefining of the gender identities in changing world.

Key words: Gender, Power, Patriarchy, Feminist, Margin

Theatre of Protest questions the hegemonic structural projections in drama, emanating from various entities—socio-cultural, economic, ethnic, racial, sex and gender, region, caste, religion and have the support of these dominant power structures. The Feminist Theatre, a part of the Theatre of Protest, is quite similar in design and structure to the Theatre of Protest as it raises voice against the patriarchal positioning in the projection of gender in drama. The genesis of the debate that male writers are not doing justice in the portrayal of woman in their body of works can be traced back to five centuries back and it got momentum with passage of time when more and more women writers as poets, novelists, playwrights, theorists, philosophers stared coming on literary horizon. Butler sums up the gendering process: 'One is not born but becomes [a woman]' and this 'becoming' involves various factors into account. While gender is something that can be improvised, it is always operating within a system of politically, culturally, and socially established norms and discursive constraints (Butler, 2004, 2). The argument by Feminist Theatre is that whatever is projected as a gender by a male writer cannot be accepted as a holy cow. Theatre generally is considered a man's territory whereas fiction is regarded more close to a woman's heart. But in the changing scenario when all these gender boundaries stand stretched and redefined and re-structured, no space or place can be labelled as exclusive and gender specific. The presence of women playwrights in the history Indian drama in English is not noteworthy; but in recent times a few women playwright in English—Poile Sengupta, Dina Mehta, Mallika Sarabhai, Usha Ganguly, Manjula Padmanabhan,, Tripurarai Sharma-have made their presence felt. They are contemporary and a common thread is discernible through their dramaturgy. The milieu they create is of urban, educated, middle class; deeply drenched in Indian family ethos their plays raise question with regard to socio-cultural mores which govern the traditional but changing Indian society.

The questions related to a woman's mind, body and heart are at the centre of the Feminist Theatre, but even then other aspects like economic independence and empowerment, her understanding of her own self and a hallow crated around her in the form of social norms get equal space. Poile Segupta like her other contemporary women playwrights remain obsessed with the plight of woman in Indian society which is overwhelmingly patriarchal in its structure and functioning. Drama is a powerful tool, as an art form as well as a socio-cultural tool to put forth one's ideas; as a performative art, drama needs space and is to be performed before the audience comprising both man and woman, and this performance at public spaces puts the performer at the centre. Elaborating on a woman acquiring the public spaces like stage, Lata Singh remarks: 'Women performers are the most public women, available to the male gaze. The performers move on to the public stage to enact what is meant to be the most private of relations.' (Singh, 256) Being women, they feel a special sort of affinity with the lives of woman, and their dramaturgy underscores the position of woman vis a vis man in Indian society. While delineating woman in various social set ups, they capture the invisible forces controlling the members of society. Gerda Lerner observes:

> 'Her [woman] indoctrination from early childhood on, emphasized her obligation not only to make an economic contribution to the kin and household but also to accept a marriage partner in line with family interests" (Lerner, 219).

Various factors like body, space colour, ethnicity, economic condition, play their part in determining the gender role of man and woman. Human history is a witness to the fact that man has been at the centre of all the affairs in this world and has enjoyed the advantageous position on account of various factors-biological, social, economic, cultural- as all these factors are controlled by man under patriarchy, putting woman to a marginalized position, as 'gendered relations are tied up with relations of power.' (Alsop, 99) Polie's *Mangalam* is a family play and has all the ingredients of a social tragedy-frustrations, deceit, ego-clashes, silent sufferings, violence (visible and invisible) sexual perversions, deceit, treachery, backdoor games, clash of generations, failures, appearance and façade—are writ large on every page and every dramatis personae-male/female. Speaking about Mangalm, Poile says "... (the) play is about family politics, seen through the perspective of women. The play deals with serrated relationships behind ostensibly normal households, whether in small town in Southern India of the 1960s, or in a modern cosmopolitan family.... It is about vulnerabilities of women across all strata of society, and in varied households, and the tenderness and spirit that is so often brutally suppressed" (Sengupta 01).

Man remains obsessed with his name and dignity in society; the patriarchal structure constructs him to have an inflated sense of self and this egoistic self gets expression in humiliation of the other gender-woman. Man is associated with his macho image, and any erosion of this image is unsettling to man. Dorai day and night goes through this mental conflict of being the husband of Manglam whose body is impure, carrying the seeds of someone. In his frustrations, he reveals his inner conflict before Thangam: '…I have lived with it for 31 years. Every moment I spent in this house, in her house, I have had to live with it. That they bought me, her family bought me to keep their good name. Her father bought me. To keep his self-respect, for his daughter's self-respect (softly, bitterly) and then, the other thing, the thing that haunts me, that robs my sleep—.'(Sengupta, 110) He feels devoid of name and self-esteem, though he has been wanton and has his own ways with women, like his father. He vents out his frustrations on his son Kannan: Your mother is dead, your whore of a sister has eloped and you come here for fees. Fees! Get out before I—' (Sengupta, 109) Despite a pervert, Dorai can't digest the decision taken by his daughter to marry the person of his choice, but he never reflects upon his doings. The revelation that his wife Mangalm carried illegitimate child jeopardizes Dorai's sense of self, and this makes him call his wife a wanton woman, without knowing the truth behind it: '…Since your parents did not tell you, let me tell you now after 31 years—your sister was pregnant when I married her. Pregnant! With another man's child.' (Sengupta, 120)

Poile by projecting two sets of families wants to show that a woman's life is full of miseries, wrongdoings; she remains the target of all sorts of violence-body and mind and soul-even by the people who are closely associated with her-family, husband, father, brother and the extender family. She is constantly living in fear of being outraged and molested. Thangam's statement 'Fear makes people remember. A woman who is afraid will never go wrong.' (Sengupta, 118) speaks of man's treatment of woman. He instills the element of fear in the psyche of woman thinking that this will allow him complete control over a woman's self. The power-drunk man remains oblivious and indifferent to what a woman craves and wants in life. Along with respect and dignity, she hopes for some soft touches as well a sense of belongingness with equal rights. The women writers on account of their gendered affiliation can feel the pulse of things happening at the hearts of a woman, and this allows Poile to bring to the fore the longings as well as multiple inward conflicts of her women characters:

> FEMALE VOICE (off): Women die many kinds of deaths; men do not know this.
>
> For them, when a woman cooks
>
> and arranges flowers in her hair
>
> and makes place in the bed
>
> she is alive. (Sengupta, 100)

Poile argues that a woman's life full of torments; she suffers for no fault of their own. Their sexuality makes them vulnerable to the men around them. Peta Bowden says: 'Women's bodies perceived to be more bodily than men's - and their minds accordingly weaker.' (Bowden, 49) Men operate like a gang to haul up women, physically, mentally, socially. She depicts men as offenders, molesters, brutal; they treat women as what Sumati calls a sexual baggage: '... means that the moment a woman doesn't fit into the category of being a mother or a sister, she's baggage (with a look at her mother); sexual baggage. (Sengupta, 129)

True to the spirit of Feminist Theatre, *Mangalam* details how woman remains a tool for sexual gratification as well as target of domestic violence and exposes the designs both of man and patriarchy in perpetuating this gender structuring where woman has to live on the mercy of man. Man is the main perpetrator of sexual crimes against woman; with power or ensnaring gulies he exploits woman physically. Dorai, his father, Thangam's husband, Nari—all are perverts and molesters. But at the same time, they are highly conscious of their social positioning and name in society. Patriarchy functions as a unit and uses woman as a toll to their advantage. Mangalam's father instead of bringing molester to the book, uses his money power to keep his family name and honour and marries off Manglam with Dorai who comes of a poor family in comparison to the Manglam's family. But the truth about Manglam's pregnancy continuously haunts him, leaving him hollow and de-capacitated. He considers Manglam responsible for his mental agony but fails to see beyond, as who is actual culprit Manglam or or his brother –in –law who raped her. Dorai stands exposed when Thangam's comments ask him to look for the other possibility: 'Did you ever think that it could have been forced on her?' (Sengupta, 122) Male as a dominant gender puts man in an exploitative and manipulative position. Vikram's discussion with Radha about Suresh reflects a typical male mindset about woman:

> Vikram: ...I feel he's [Suresh]grown rather careless about his friendships, especially with women...He treats them

> like pieces in a chess game—... and then, once he's...
>
> Radha: Once he's had his way with them, he's not interested any more?
>
> Vikram: Yes. As if that's all there is to a relationship, as if between a man and a woman, there's only the possibility of a check and a mate. A game. A sexual conquest. (Sengupta, 145)

All the women except Revathy are victims of the patriarchal discriminative establishments, and the bruises are very much visible on their bodies as well as on their minds. But Poile presents them as conscious of the wrongs done to them but the way they respond id different from men. They remain silent and uninvolved, going through the motions in life, and this silence is a strategy adopted by woman to resists the oppressive structure emanating from age old patriarchal structures. Indu Pandey says: 'The feminist theatre ... has given voice to the silence, reconstructed the traditional images of women and presented them on stage.' (Pandey, 47-48) Woman's mind being the harbor all the violations of her body, soul and spirit, she keeps a façade of a contended exterior but deep down in their hearts they are very conscious of the horrible things done to them, as becomes obvious from Thangam's remarks to Dorai: 'A bit of rain won't kill anyone. It is the yuddha inside the house that's killing.' (Sengupta, 117) The recurrent FEMALE VOICE aptly sums up the position of woman in Indian society:

> The great silence of tragedy I can bear, the heavy weight of grief, but fate pinches me like a stubborn child, hurts me like a small time thief.... in a woman's mind, small is significant,... (Sengupta, 101)

Silence and indifference are the two potent ways adopted by woman to express her dissent or protest, and Polie has used this technique effectively through her protagonist Manglam. Silence is one of the greatest techniques adopted by woman to express her protest. Mangalam the most talked about character is present in-absentia, after her death. Despite her absence, like her silence when she was very much alive, Manglam seems presence in every line in the back of very character's mind:

> FEMALE VOICE (off): Because a woman has patience,
>
> She is not allowed to speak;
>
> Others speak for her,
>
> And she never learns the words. (Sengupta, 123)

Mangalam questions the established paradigm of gender construction which is overwhelmingly inclined in favour of man. The play juxtaposes the stereotyped projection of gender on the one hand and at the same time rejects it with alternative. Even the stratagem of introducing play-within-the play by Poile has a design of rejecting the traditional dramatic devices. Polie's use of the play-within-the play technique in *Mangalam* evokes Shakespeare's Hamlet where the playwright wants to expose what lies at the back of mind of his characters. The later part in the play is a departure from the former; whereas the traditional family set up and social mores characterize the first Act, in the second Act the seeds of modernity and change are very much visible. But one thing remains common throughout the play is the subversive tactics adopted by the male characters to keep woman at their places. Gayatri Spivak describing the working of centre-margin power games elaborates that a '...cultural identity is thrust upon one because the centre wants an identifiable margin, claims for marginality assure validation from the centre' (Spivak, 55) Those at the helm of the affairs use many strategies to keep the things under control and favourable.

Body and space are the two important signifiers determining one's gender role and identity. A man's body is viewed differently from that of a woman's; a woman is a walking spectacle on account of her bodily markers. Woman because of her physicality invites attention from man and becomes a target of what Mulvey describes male gaze: 'In a world ordered by sexual imbalance, pleasure in looking has been split between active/male and passive/female. The determining male gaze projects its fantasy on to the female figure which is styled accordingly.' (Mulvey, 837) A woman's predicament is captured in the following lines: Revathy is very conscious of her beauty and feels proud that her husband is very loyal to her. She puts the assertive Thangam at her place with her comments: 'Jealous of my beauty, jealous because my husband does not look at other women, because he strokes my head when it hurts, because he takes me to the cinema, buys me flowers. What did your husband do? He didn't come near you even on your wedding night. You don't even know what it is to have a man's arms around you. You're just a barren woman. (Sengupta, 118) So, body becomes a tool to invite attention, and also a sight where innumerable battles are fought. These physical attributes of a woman become the centre of man's voyeurism. Beauvoir describes the trauma felt by a woman when her body is scanned in public spaces: "The young girl feels that her body is getting away from her... on the street men follow her with their eyes and comment on her anatomy. She would like to be invisible; it frightens her to become flesh and to show flesh" (Beauvoir, 333). A woman's sexuality leaves her vulnerable to patriarchy to exploit. Svati Shah says that 'All women (on the street) are subject to, public moral scrutiny which evaluates women along binaries of good/bad, honourable/dishonourable, promiscuous/safe, etc.' (Shah, 234) In Manglam both Manglam the protagonist and Sumati have to face sexual onslaught by those who are very close to them on account of their sexuality:

> Because a woman has breasts,
>
> she can not be on her own;
>
> age turns her skin to parchment, and then she is left alone. (Sengupta, 123)

Cixous unsettles the patriarchy by exposing man's designs in using woman's body : 'We've been turned away from our bodies, shamefully taught to ignore them, to strike them with that stupid sexual modesty; we've been made victims of the old fool's game: each one will love the other sex. I'll give you your body and you'll give me mine. But who are the men who give women the body that women blindly yield to them?' (Cixous, 885) Space as a signifier has always remained a decisive signifier in locating the gender determining structures. While man controlled the public spaces, woman were confined to the private spaces, and even these private spaces, which should have been of their own, giving a feeling of belongingness and sense of security, become a hotbed for their exploitation. The majority of domestic violence takes place behind the curtains and in the so-called safe precincts of private spaces.

Language has its own gender; Woolf says a sentence can be labeled as a masculine and feminine. In Mangalm also Poile allows her character to make use a specific kind of language which crosses the gender boundaries. Traditionally, woman is supposed to be soft, decent, persuasive and enticing while selecting words; her tone is bereft of any kind of authority or control. But here Thangam's preference for certain words defies the traditional gender constructing process. She is very direct, candid and nonplussed in using language which only man uses in a patriarchal structure: 'A woman who opens her mouth and smiles at men will also open her legs.' (Sengupta, 118) So what? Cutting Dorai to his size she further remarks: Did you tell her the names of the women you had slept with? What abput that married woman who used to come to the temple every day and take prasaadam from your father? She took prasaadam from you also, didn't she? (Sengupta, 121) Even Dorai admits this, and puts man at a different pedestal so far morality is concerned: 'It's different for a man.' (Sengupta, 121) Even Sumati doesn't feel shy of speaking about her mind in a manner which may sound outrageous to man: 'A woman who allows herself to be soft, who relinquishes her weapons...well she gets chewed up, doesn't she? I know it's a terrible expression, but then it's a terrible state to be in...'

(Sengupta, 148-49) A woman does not speak out her mind to communicate; one has to observe her behaviour, kinesics and body language to know what is going through her mind or what she wants. She always communicates indirectly, dropping hints here and there. While hinting at Mangalam's past and pregnancy, Dorai tells Thangam: 'You know your sister. She never said anything directly. But once or twice, she hinted at it.' (98) But Thangam forces him to face the reality that it is men like him who keep woman silent and don't allow them to express: 'You made her do that. She was afraid of you. My poor sister. She was afraid of you. Don't I know it? You are a raakshasan. A Kali-yuga raakshasan. (Sengupta, 98)

The forces at the centre in gender construction process use all sorts of stratagems to keep the 'other'-woman- at the periphery. One who enjoys the power controls the naming process, and this gives unchecked power in the hands of man to name woman as per to his whims. Mary Daly observes about the gender conflict: 'The sexist society maintains its grip over the psyche by keeping it divided against itself.' (Daly, 128) The women toeing the line of patriarchy are bestowed with name and dignity while those questioning the powers that be are derided and inflicted indignities. Rekha observes how the gender construction process favours man because it is the man who determines the position of woman in society; the conforming are eulogized with a patronizing attitude while those defying these gender roles are ridiculed, mocked and vilified in public domain : 'Woman as conforming entity'—Those who conform are idealized, while those who deviate or resist, personify normative fissures, and tensions or embody ambiguities and thus produce unstable results, are demonized.' (Rekha, 11) Dorai's patriarchal mindset never allows him to accept the marriage of his daughter Chitra with a Non-Brahmin boy. Chitra's decision of marriage with a boy of her own choice not only questions Dorai's authority but also sullies Dorai's image as per his own admission: '... my daughters are prostitutes!...The whole town is laughing at me. …Look what has happened now. Like a curse.' (Sengupta, 108)

In Indian society a widow is always an unwelcome and looked down upon not only bay man only bit the entire society because man even controls the interiors of woman, and they think only what the patriarchy wants them to think. Dorai's sharp comments are representative of this patriarchal mindset: 'I will not allow a shaven head to fix my child's marriage! That woman will leave my house immediately.' (Sengupta, 99) Motherhood is considered as the essence of a woman's existence; one who can't become a mother is not only derided by man only, but even by woman as well, without even knowing the truth whether fault lies with man or woman. Dorai mocks Thangam as well as her husband: '…And what happened to you? You were married to an engineer in a big firm. What did he leave you? He drank everything. He couldn't' even give you a child, that eunuch, that— '(Sengupta, 100) Even Ravathy, a woman, takes a jibe at Thangam for not becoming a mother and calls her a …'barren, jealous woman. (Sengupta, 119) Even Thangam the most vocal character in the play admits that the society treats man and woman differently. She says 'It's different for a man.' (148) The traditional Indian value system accepts this dichotomy of difference in gender roles but the modern, free thinking young Indian society, depicted in the second part of the play protests against this discrimination of putting man in a privileged position: But Sumati's vitriolic outbursts shows the generational change who cannot accept the special status bestowed on man: 'How? How can it be different? In marriage, how can it be different? Outside marriage, yes. The man seems to have all the advantages. He can have a roaring good time and he can pick and choose and drop and choose again. But once he's into a marriage, he's just as involved, isn't he? Just as vulnerable.' (Sengupta, 148)

The construction and perpetuation of binaries—good/bad, white/ black, urban/rural, modern/traditional, man/woman, west/east, occidental/oriental, centre/margin, dignified/loose, pure/impure—

have a design behind it. Those enjoying powers have control over this process. The binaries negate the possibility of alternates, and this serves the purpose of those calling shots in the power games. The gender roles are dissecting from man/woman perspective, and that also from a patriarchal standpoint. In Mangalm, the positioning of all the characters seem to be divided on gender lines; men enjoying power over women, and exercising their authority over the latter while women, denied of space, place, name, identity appear helpless, frustrated, and pathetic because of men's callousness and insensitivity. But a gradual change is discernible from beginning to the end, and this change in the position of woman- from submissive to aware, subdued to indifference, from resignation to protest man resistance—is central to Poile's dramaturgy in the present play. Chitra is not Mangalam, Sumita is different from Thangam while Revathy having her own self charters her own territory within her family unit. Mary Douglas exposes how binaries are manipulated against women: 'By defining women by the pure/impure binary, 'men could render them relatively harmless', blunting their male challenge to male privillege'. (Douglas, p.36) Thangam, Sumati and Revathy are presented as conscious woman; they resist the existing gender structure in their own way. They refuse to toe the line of male world directly but try to walk on unchartered territory. Poile in Mangalam exposes the existing hierarchies in gender roles and asks for re-writing and re-defining of these gender identities. Through her stanza off stage Poile conveys her message about a woman's perseverance and determination in life; she as been depicted as a source of strength that can hold the world together, something a man can't do:

And there will be storms
And the wind will blow very strong
But the women will stay, like trees,
They will hold the world together. (151)

Works Cited:

Alsop, Rachel et al. theorizing gender: Judith Butler: 'The Queen of Queer'. Oxford: Blackwell Pub. 2002.

Bowden, Peta). Understanding Feminism II Embodiment. New York: Routledge, 2009.

Butler, Judith. Undoing Gender. New York: Routledge, 2004.

Beauvoir, Simon de. The Second Sex, Trans. and Ed, H.M. Parshley. London: Vintage, 1997.

Cixous, Helene, et al. (1976). 'The Laugh of Medusa', Chicago Journals.Signs, Vol. 1, No. 4 (Summer, 1976), pp. 875-893 Published by: The University of Chicago Press Stable URL: http://www.jstor.org/stable/3173239 Accessed: 22/04/2009 14:57

Daly, Mary. Beyond God the Father. Boston: Beacon, 1973.

Lerner, Gerda. The Creation of Patriarchy. Oxford University Press, NY, 1986.

Douglas, Mary. Purity and Danger: An Analysis of Concepts of Purity and Taboo. New York: Routledge, 1966

Mulvey, Laura. "Visual Pleasure and Narrative Cinema." Film Theory and Criticism : Introductory Readings. Eds. Leo Braudy and Marshall Cohen. New York: Oxford UP, 1999 (pp.,833-44).

Pandey, Indu. "Female Playwrights and the Theatre in India: Challenges and Perspectives." Bharatiya Prajna: An Interdisciplinary Journal of Indian Studies. Murshidabad, West Bengal: 1.1 (2016) 47–52. Print.

Rekha. Gender, Space and Imagination: The Poetics and Politics of Women's Writing in India. New Delhi: Primus Books, 2015.

Sengupta, Poile. Body Blows: Women, Violence and Survival: Three Plays. Calcutta: Seagull Books, 2000.

——————. Women Centre Stage. Routledge Publication, 2010.

Shah, Svati, (2003). ' Soliciting" on a Mumbai Street Corner: Work, Sex and Gender', paper presented at City One: South Asian Conference on the Urban Experience, Sarai @ Centre for the Study of Developing Societies (CSDS), New Delhi, January.

Singh, Lata . "Women in Theatre: Journey from Respectability to Agency" Thinking Gender, Doing Gender: Feminist Scholarship and Practice Today. Ed. Uma Chakravarti. New Delhi: Orient BlackSwan, 2016.

Spivak, Gayatri Chakravorty. Outside in the Teaching Machine. New York: Routledge, 1993.

9. The Evolution of the Portrayal of Women in Indian Literature and Media: A Study of Ancient, Medieval and Modern Representations

Dr Seema Gupta

Abstract: Women have played a significant role in Indian mythology, modern India, and the world. Their representation and portrayal, however, have been diverse and complex, reflecting the cultural, religious, and societal norms and expectations that have shaped the respective societies throughout history. In Indian literature, the portrayal of women has evolved over time, reflecting the changing societal attitudes towards women. In ancient Indian literature such as the Vedas and the Epics, women were often portrayed as powerful and respected figures. In medieval Indian literature, such as the Puranas and the Bhakti literature, women were often depicted as submissive and dependent on men. In modern Indian literature, the portrayal of women has become more nuanced and diverse. For example, in the works of contemporary Indian authors such as Arundhati Roy, Jhumpa Lahiri, and Chitra Banerjee Divakaruni, women are portrayed as strong and independent individuals with their own goals and aspirations. However, in popular Indian literature, such as the works of Chetan Bhagat, the portrayal of women is often stereotypical and traditional, with female characters being limited in terms of their agency and autonomy.

In Indian media, the representation of women has also evolved over time. For example, in early Indian cinema, women were often portrayed as submissive and dependent on men. However, in recent years, there has been a shift towards more positive and empowering portrayals of women in Indian cinema. For example, in films such as *Queen* (2013), *Pink* (2016) and *Lipstick Under My Burkha* (2016) women are depicted as strong and independent individuals who challenge societal norms and expectations. The present paper will examine the representation of women in Indian literature and media, starting from ancient times to the modern era. This paper also aims to explore and compare the presentation and challenges faced by women in Indian mythology, modern India, and the world.

Keywords: Strong, Independent, Subservient, Mythology, Religious

The evolution of portrayal of women in Indian literature and media has undergone significant changes over the centuries. From ancient scriptures and epics to contemporary works, women have been depicted in diverse ways, reflecting the social, cultural, and political changes in Indian society. The present paper will examine the representation of women in Indian literature and media, starting from ancient times to the modern era. This paper also aims to explore and compare the presentation and challenges faced by women in Indian mythology, modern India, and the world.

In Indian mythology, women have been portrayed as powerful goddesses with significant roles in the natural and supernatural world. The earliest texts of Indian mythology, such as the Rigveda and the Upanishads, depict goddesses like Saraswati and Kali as powerful and influential figures. Saraswati, the goddess of knowledge, arts, and learning, is revered as the embodiment of wisdom, while Kali, the goddess of destruction, is considered to be a powerful and destructive force. These goddesses are revered and worshipped by many, and their depiction in mythology serves as an inspiration for many women in India.

However, as Indian society became more patriarchal over time, the portrayal of women in mythology began to shift. In the epic poems of the *Mahabharata* and the Ramayana, women are often relegated to secondary roles and are depicted as subservient to men. For example, in the *Mahabharata*, Draupadi, the wife of the five Pandavas, is humiliated and disrobed in front of a court of men, while in the Ramayana, Sita, the wife of Rama, is forced to prove her chastity through a test of fire. These negative portrayals of women in mythology reflect the societal norms and expectations of women in ancient India, which often emphasized chastity and obedience.

In addition to these negative portrayals, there are also positive examples of women in Indian mythology who are strong and independent. For example, in the Devi Mahatmya, a Hindu text, the goddess Durga is portrayed as a fierce warrior who defeats the demon Mahishasura. The goddess Parvati who is the consort of Lord Shiva, is also depicted as a powerful and independent goddess.

Additionally, many goddesses in Indian mythology are also considered as the embodiment of various aspects of femininity such as fertility, motherhood, and sensuality. The goddesses such as Laxmi, Durga and Kali are also considered as the protectors and nurturers of their devotees.

Moving on to modern India, women have made significant progress in terms of education, employment, and political participation. However, they still face significant societal and cultural barriers, particularly in terms of gender discrimination, domestic violence, and sexual harassment. According to data from the World Bank, the literacy rate among Indian women has increased from around 54% in 2001 to around 65% in 2016. Additionally, the enrollment of girls in primary and secondary education has also increased in recent years. In terms of employment, women in India have also made progress, particularly in urban areas, with the female labour force participation rate is increasing from around 27% in 1990 to around 29% in 2019.

On the global scale, women throughout the world have made

significant progress in recent decades in terms of education, employment, and political participation. However, they still face significant barriers, particularly in terms of gender discrimination and violence. According to data from the United Nations, the literacy rate among women has increased from around 80% in 2000 to around 86% in 2018. Additionally, the enrollment of girls in primary and secondary education has also increased in recent years. In terms of employment, women have also made progress globally, with the female labor force participation rate increasing from around 52% in 1990 to around 57% in 2019. However, women still face significant barriers in the workforce, such as discrimination and a lack of affordable childcare. In terms of political participation, women have also made progress in recent years, with the number of women in parliament increasing in many countries, and there have been several high-profile female politicians throughout the world. However, women still face significant barriers to political participation, such as discrimination and a lack of resources.

Despite these similarities, there are also significant differences in terms of the barriers faced by modern women in India and modern women throughout the world. For example, Indian women face a higher risk of domestic violence and sexual harassment than women in many other countries. Additionally, India has a widespread problem with gender discrimination and a lack of legal protections for women, which is a significant barrier for Indian women.

The topic of the paper"The Evolution of the Portrayal of Women in Indian Literature and Media: A Study of Ancient, Medieval and Modern Representations" is vast and complex, with many different aspects to consider. One specific aspect that can be explored is the portrayal and representation of women in Indian literature and media, and how this reflects and influences societal attitudes towards women. In Indian literature, the portrayal of women has evolved over time, reflecting the changing societal attitudes towards women. However, as Indian society became more patriarchal over time, the portrayal of women in literature began to shift. Just as in ancient Indian literature such as the Vedas and the Epics, women were often portrayed as powerful and respected figures, in medieval Indian literature, such as the Puranas and the Bhakti literature, women were often depicted as submissive and dependent on men. For example, in the Bhagavata Purana, Radha, a devotee of Lord Krishna, is depicted as a submissive and dependent woman who is deeply in love with Lord Krishna. Similarly, in Bhakti literature, women are often portrayed as devoted and submissive wives and mothers.

However, in modern Indian literature, the portrayal of women has become more nuanced and diverse. For example, in the works of contemporary Indian authors such as Arundhati Roy, Jhumpa Lahiri, and Chitra Banerjee Divakaruni, women are portrayed as strong and independent individuals with their own goals and aspirations. However, in popular Indian literature, such as the works of Chetan Bhagat, the portrayal of women is often stereotypical and traditional, with female characters being limited in terms of their agency and autonomy.

In Indian media, the representation of women has also evolved over time. For example, in early Indian cinema, women were often portrayed as submissive and dependent on men. However, in recent years, there has been a shift towards more positive and empowering portrayals of women in Indian cinema. For example, in films such as *Queen* (2013), *Pink* (2016) and *Lipstick Under My Burkha* (2016) women are depicted as strong and independent individuals who challenge societal norms and expectations. Modern women face a wide range of challenges in today's society. One of the most significant challenges is discrimination and bias in the workplace. Despite progress in recent decades, women still face barriers to advancement and are underrepresented in leadership positions. They are often paid less than men for doing the same job, a phenomenon known as the gender pay gap.

Another major challenge for women is the struggle to balance work and family responsibilities. Women are still expected to take on the majority of caregiving responsibilities, whether it's for children, aging parents, or other family members. This can make it difficult for women to fully participate in the workforce and can limit their career advancement opportunities.

Women also continue to experience harassment and violence in their daily lives. This can take many forms, from verbal and physical abuse to sexual harassment and assault. It can occur in the workplace, in public spaces, and even in the home. This can make it difficult for women to feel safe and secure, and can have a negative impact on their mental and physical health. Societal pressure for women to conform to traditional gender roles and beauty standards can also be a challenge. Women are often judged and evaluated based on their appearance, and are expected to meet certain societal expectations about how they should look and behave. This can be stressful and can lead to feelings of self-doubt and inadequacy.

Women also face unique health concerns, such as reproductive health issues. These issues can include lack of access to affordable and comprehensive healthcare, as well as societal attitudes that stigmatize certain aspects of reproductive health. This can make it difficult for women to get the care they need, which can have serious consequences for their overall health and wellbeing.

There are a variety of solutions that can help address the challenges faced by modern women. One solution to discrimination and bias in the workplace is to promote diversity and inclusion initiatives. This can include things like mentoring programs for women, as well as initiatives to increase the representation of women in leadership positions. Additionally, implementing policies such as family leave and flexible work arrangements can help support women in balancing work and family responsibilities. Another solution to the issue of harassment and violence is to create a culture of consent and respect. This can include education and training programs for employees and students, as well as clear policies and procedures for addressing and preventing harassment and assault. Additionally, providing support and resources for survivors can help them to heal and move forward.

To reduce societal pressure for women to conform to traditional gender roles and beauty standards, it is important to promote positive body image and self-esteem. This can include things like media literacy education and campaigns that promote diversity and acceptance of all body types. To address unique health concerns, it is important to increase access to affordable and comprehensive healthcare for women. This can include policies such as Medicaid expansion and the Affordable Care Act, as well as initiatives to increase the number of women in healthcare professions. It's also important to address the cultural and societal attitudes that stigmatize certain aspects of reproductive health and make it difficult for women to access the care they need.

Reputed thinkers like Gayatri Chakravorty Spivak and Kumkum Sangari have written extensively on the representation of women in Indian literature and media. Spivak, in her essay *Can the Subaltern Speak?* explores the ways in which power and oppression intersect to silence marginalized groups, including women. Sangari, in her book *Politics of the Possible*, examines the role of popular culture in reinforcing patriarchal norms and the limitations of feminist resistance in the face of these norms.

Chitra Divakaruni, who has explored the experiences of Indian women in the diaspora in her works, including the novel *Mistress of Spices*. Shobha De, who has written about the lives and struggles of modern Indian women in her novels and articles. Bapsi Sidhwa, who has explored the experiences of women from different ethnic and religious communities in India in her novels, including *Cracking India*.

Ruth Vanita, who has written extensively on the representation of same-sex love and desire in Indian literature and history. Uma Chakravarti, who has written on the role of women in Indian history, including the study "Gendering Caste Through a Feminist Lens." These scholars and writers have all made important contributions to the ongoing conversation about the portrayal of women in Indian literature and media. Their works have helped to shed light on the ways in which patriarchal norms and gender-based violence impact the lives of women in India, and have inspired ongoing efforts to work towards a more nuanced and empowering representation of women in Indian literature and media.

At the end, the portrayal of women in Indian literature and media has evolved throughout history, reflecting the changing attitudes and beliefs of Indian society. However, harmful stereotypes and patriarchal norms persist, and the representation of women in Indian media often perpetuates these norms. Further exploration and analysis by scholars and feminists are necessary to understand the full extent of the impact of these representations and to work towards a more nuanced and empowering representation of women in Indian literature and media. Addressing the challenges faced by modern women requires a multifaceted approach. It requires creating an inclusive culture in workplaces, promoting policies such as family leave and flexible work arrangements and implementing education and training programs to combat harassment and violence. Additionally, promoting positive body image and self-esteem, increasing access to healthcare and addressing cultural and societal attitudes that stigmatize certain aspects of reproductive health can also help to empower and support women.

Works Cited:

Chakravarti, U. (1993). Gendering Caste Through a Feminist Lens. New Delhi: Kali for Women.

De, S. (1980). Socialite Evenings. New Delhi: Penguin Books India.

Divakaruni, C. (1997). Mistress of Spices. New Delhi: Anchor Books.

Sangari, K. (1990). Politics of the Possible: Essays on Gender, History, Narratives, Colonial English. New Delhi: Kali for Women.

Sidhwa, B. (1991). Cracking India. New Delhi: Penguin Books India.
Spivak, G.C. (1988). Can the Subaltern Speak? In Marxism and the Interpretation of Culture (pp. 271-313). Basingstoke: Macmillan Education.
Vanita, R. (1992). Love's Rite: Same-Sex Love and the Path to Cultural Change. New Delhi: Penguin Books India.

10. Portrayal of Class Struggle and Exploitation in *In Dubious Battle*

Dr Nirmal Atri

Abstract: Marxism is a theoretical framework that emphasizes the struggle between social classes and the exploitation of the working class by the ruling class. According to Marxism, the capitalist class, which owns the means of production, exploits the working class by paying them low wages and keeping the surplus value generated by their labour. The working class, on the other hand, is oppressed and alienated from their work and their social existence. *In Dubious Battle*, written by John Steinbeck, is a novel that portrays the labour movement during the Great Depression era. The novel tells the story of Jim Nolan, a young man who joins a group of apple pickers in California to fight for their rights and demand better working conditions. A Marxist analysis of the novel reveals that it highlights the struggle between the working class and the capitalist class, the exploitation of the workers and the importance of collective action.

Keywords: Marxism, Class and Production.

Introduction: The concept of classes and class struggle is central to Marxist theory. Since the day man progressed from the stage of primitive communism, there has been a fierce competition among different classes for the control over the means of production. The class that won the battle controlled the economic structure and thereby superstructure and imposed its ideas on the rest of the society, made laws, created religion, evolved a political system to serve its interests. According to Marx and Engels, industrialization created division and conflict between two classes, bourgeois and proletarian i.e., those who own the means of production and those who work for the owners. The interests between the two classes are always in conflict, where the former group benefits at the expense of workers. The bourgeoisie rule the capitalist society by owning the means of production, and in order for the proletariat to survive they are forced to sell their labour power (Marx and Engels, chapter 2-4). It is through the capitalist mode of production that exploitation emerges. According to Marx, the capitalist exploits the workers by paying them less than they deserve, or by providing them with a poorer work environment than required and so on. By exploiting the worker, the capitalist is able to get more surplus value than is otherwise achievable (Marx and Engels, 242- 243). According to Arun Boss, it is through the exploitation that alienation develops (Bose, 10). This exploitation of one social class by another is seen especially in modern industrial capitalism of 19th century. Alienation occurs, when the worker is disliked and made to perform fragmented, repetitive tasks in a sequence of whose nature and purpose he or she has no overall grasp, whereas in the older cottage industry system of manufacturing, home and workplace were one. Workers are bereft of their full humanity and are thought of as hands or labour force, in other words, people are reduced to things (Berry, 157).

Karl Marx had a broader and more scientific view of exploitation, i. e. the forced appropriation of unpaid labour of workers. According to this definition, all working class people are exploited. And because exploitation is the root cause of capitalism, the only way to get rid of exploitation is to achieve a totally different society i.e., socialist society where there is no tiny minority to rule the major section of the society. It is the concept of classes and class conflicts that constitute the core of Marxist ideology.

Marxist Analysis of *In Dubious Battle*:

John Steinbeck describes the conflict between classes as the hard work and low wages, the workers are forced to accept in order to survive. The novelist is against the exploitation of workers and its consequences. Although the rich land owners depend on the labour class for their productivity but want the cost to be as low as possible by keeping the wages down and thus creating a conflict. He wrote his famous novels *In Dubious Battle*, Of Mice and Men, and The Grapes of Wrath during a difficult period in American history. The Great Depression had a major impact on American society. According to Gerald D. Nash, 33% of work force became unemployed and many were forced to migrate around the country in search of job (Nash, 6-7). Through his writings, the novelist suggests that the society dominated by capitalists alienate and suffer human beings. Most of his novels can be described as critique of capitalism. During 1920s, in California, capitalism actually walked along with industrialism. As discussed by Marx, the effect of this development is the shift of surplus value, where capitalists, as the dominant class, take away the massive profit from this economic change. The working class unites against the capitalists in economic matters especially concerning wages. Class struggle then becomes the motive behind the social revolution. Watts says that Steinbeck is harshly critical of capitalists (Watts, The Businessmen in American Literature, 92). He has used migrants as a weapon of protest. But it should be noted that he attacks the excesses of capitalism during the Great Depression era and not the system itself. His main concern is humanistic and humanitarian. Steinbeck's criticism mainly targets big businessmen such as rich landlords and bankers. The novelist criticizes the capitalists for their control over poor people's lives and their exploitation of cheap labour as well as their illegal and shoddy business practices. Moreover, the novelist was keenly aware of the economic changes taking place during his times as well as small farms were vanishing because big corporate farms owned by the big businessmen and bankers were emerging. Agricultural industrialization divided farmers. In his essay "Dubious Battle in California" in 1936, he observes that not all the farmers belong to the same class:

> There are in California, therefore, two distinct classes of farmers widely separated in standard of living, desires, needs and sympathies; the very small farmers who more often than not take the sides of workers in disputes and speculative farmers.

Steinbeck has used the body of hungry migrant workers and their hungry children, including a stillborn baby, to protest the miserable living and working conditions of the migrants and to warn the inevitability of a revolution by the dispossessed and oppressed. Steinbeck exposes more than any other writer of his generation, the exploitation, oppression and problems of migrants during the Great Depression in his novels.

In Dubious Battle can be considered as John Steinbeck's first major novel about socio-economic and political issues of that time as it deals with a strike of migrants in California's apple orchard. The Great Depression influenced to a great extent the writings of the novelists and criticized the social environment. This novel is important as it inspired the writer to write other novels having the same theme i.e criticizing the social conditions. It represents the novelist's idea of the conflicts between bourgeois and working class, and the interference of communist party. In this novel Steinbeck focuses on the issue of capitalists and communist exploitation of workers. The title of the novel *In Dubious Battle* itself refers to the quotation from Milton's Paradise Lost in which the term is used to describe the revolt of Satan against God. This reference points out the analogies between the war in heaven and the strike in California, particularly between characters in the human and cosmic conflicts (French, xx). The only similarity between these battles is that both are dubious, unnecessary and unjustified. "What is in doubt is not who will win but why the opponents should ever come to blows...the struggle in Steinbeck's novel is over how the profits from cultivating the fruits of the earth shall be shared by the participants in the process..." (French, xxi).

The novel focuses on the exploitation and discrimination towards migrants by the bourgeoisie and encourages the readers to strike against the injustices towards poor and less fortunate people. *In Dubious Battle*, the strikers' cause is justifiable one; the rich owners wait for the migrant fruit pickers until they reach California after selling their belongings and putting themselves to the trouble of coming there. Then they are informed that the wages promised to them for the work are to be lowered as the workers are more in number. Sometimes the fruit tramps are cought and forced to do the picking in order to make up the loss. The owners gamble on this and go on forcing people to do the picking for them without paying any wages to them and poor migrants have no alternative but to make only a feeble protest. Although the workers want better wages, but they do nothing till Jim and Mac, the workers of Communist party, come to Torgas Valley from San Francisco to make these people aware about their rights and stir them into life. Of course, the strike restores some of their confidence; thousands of them have been roused to resistance, and even though they engage in a dubious battle i.e. their strike may be lost, it will have its impact on other fronts. Workers learn important lessons from the strike as they come to know about the methods used by the owners to cheat them in the matter of wages; how they induce some workers to spy on their fellow workers, hire bullies to beat up the strikers and even stoop to murder by ambush. The novelist brings life back to these poor migrants who had lost their confidence and living like zombies, through the efforts of Mac and Jim. They organise workers, even built a small camp on the land of the sympathizers to their cause. Mac also gets his friend, a doctor, to come to the Valley and supervise hygienic preparations so that these poor workers should not be ordered off the land on technicality. Irrigation ditches were dug, housewives donate some material to make tents with; they even get some old stoves and other articles for the migrants. And then strikers and their families move in and a sense of community is created. On one occasion, Mac plays a role of midwife and helped delivering a grandchild of London, a man who was considered as the head of the loosely organized bands of migrants. Mac and Jim are Communist party workers referred to 'reds' in the novel, seem to be on good terms with labourers, have their own interests, and hegemonize the workers through propaganda to start the rebellion. MAC says,"Down the Torgas Valley, there are thousands of acres of apples ready to pick down there. Be damn near two thousand fruit tramps. Well, the Growers' Association just announced a pay cut to the pickers. They'll be sore as hell. If we can get a ruckus going down there we might be able to spread it to the cotton fields in Tandale" (In Dubious Battle, p. 36).

Actually, the novelist wants to show the greed of human beings and their ambitions to take control over others thus making the bourgeoisie richer in the process. The Growers Association is bent upon making profit even at the cost of poor migrants – capitalizing on the poor fruit pickers' inability to make long trips into the town for grocery items after the tiresome work in the fields. They are compelled to buy the food from the stores owned by rich land owners at a very high price, almost at a day's wages. Jim Nolan finds about this when he was talking to a fruit picker named Dan. As Dan makes his way from the fields, he tells Jim:

> "Guess I'll go over to the store and get me a can of beans. These damn fools pay seventeen cents for a pound of canned beans. Why, they could get four pounds of canned beans for that, and cooked up that'd make nearly eight pounds...women work all day, men work all day; and the owner charges three cents extra for a can of beans because the men are too damn tired to go into town for groceries" (In Dubious Battle, p. 77).

Though Dan is aware of inflated prices at the store, still he does not have any alternative but to go to the store and buy a can of beans as he is too damn tired to go into town for groceries. The Growers Association purposefully keeps the prices high and poor workers impoverished in order to earn more profit. They use media such as newspaper, propaganda, law etc. to scare the powerless people. The novelist uses Marxist theory in the hegemony perspective. Although the landowners pay fewer wages to the workers, they still want to control them. Gramisci states that, "hegemony is political but also and above all economic, it has its material base in the decisive function exercised by the hegemonic group in the decisive core of economic activity" (Gramisci, 461). One who hegemonize the working class in the novel are the rich landlords and the Communist party workers Mac and Jim, referred to as 'reds' in the novel. The characters that are hegemonized are people in the society, including both the citizens and all the apple pickers on the farm. Both the ideological and repressive ways are used by the landowners to gain control over the society. They use law to make people obedient to it, cops, sheriff's to control over lower class people and the media to hegemonize the rest of the citizens, and to gain control over public opinion not to participate in strike against the landowners.

Propaganda is also used in the novel as a medium of counter hegemony to hegemonize the workers. Jim and Mac influence the workers through several ways. First they try to create good image as the saviour of poor workers as it helps them gain people's attention and trust towards them. Mac offers tobacco to a group of apple pickers as they were sitting and talking. He "... pulled out his sack of tobacco and made a careful, excellent cigarette; then as an afterthought, 'Would any of you capitalists like a smoke?' several hands thrust out. The bag went from man to man" (In Dubious Battle, p.57). As they start talking, the workers tell Mac that they have been offered only fifteen cents for picking apples. Mac advises them not to pick the apples because, "if we don't pick'em, they'll rot" (p.57). It is clear that Mac is telling them to go on strike. Both Mac and Jim encourage poor workers through their speech and language. They are good orators and people easily agree with them. Next, they influence people by showing them that there is an inspiring leader to follow. They can hegemonize the people through propaganda. On the other hand, the people who possess the ruling system such as landowners, they could do anything, even killing someone whoever opposed them, to gain control over people.

The town vigilantes are depicted as another destructive phalanx. They victimize the poor migrants on behalf of rich landlords. Instead of maintaining law and order and helping the poor workers, they bully them, threaten them and even beat them without any reason. There is a newspaper clipping describing the Town Vigilantes' ideology:

> We (the town) believe the time has come to take action. When transient labourers tie up the Valley's most important industry, when fruit tramps, led and inspired by paid foreign agitators (that's us Jim), carry on a campaign of violence, and burning, bringing Red Russia into peaceful America, when our highways are no longer safe for American citizens, nor their homes safe from firebrands, we believe the time for action has come" (In Dubious Battle, p. 298).

Through this appeal to extremist ideology, the conflict between the town and the strikers is amplified from a baby strike for wages at local level into a political battle between "Red Russia and a once peaceful America" no longer safe for American citizens. Vigilantes burn a farmhouse, destroy a sympathizer's business place, and murder Jim outside strikers' camp. As Jim says:

> Why, they're the dirtiest guys in any town. They are the same ones that burned the houses of old German people during the war. They're the same ones that lynch Negroes. They like to be cruel. They like to hurt people, and they always give it a nice name, patriotism or protecting the constitution…" (In Dubious Battle, p. 172).

Even though the strikers are presented as being taken advantage of and abused throughout the novel, they are also made into a destructive phalanx. Mac and Jim have voluntarily given up their individuality for the sake of the party's goals that make the strikers' phalanx a failure. These two men force their views upon the workers instead of encouraging democratic and creative participation. Mac coercively guides the strike and tells a worker:

> "...nominate London, here, for chairman. They'll put him in all right. They'll do almost anything. That's all you got to do, Sam…Now listen, London, soon's you're, chairman, you tell'em we got to have order. You give'em a list of guys, about ten, and tell'em to vote for these guys as a committee to figure things out" (In Dubious Battle, p. 108).

In this way, taking any decision in a democratic way, he takes the election in his own hands and manipulates the structure of the protest to his will. He is manipulating rather than including the workers coupled with party's goals instead of workers' interests, corrupting the phalanx. The result is it becomes violent. Under the control of Mac and Jim, workers go to a nearby orchard and scare the replaced workers that have taken their jobs. In their fury, strikers lower themselves to the level of cruel Vigilantes engaging in the same kind of violence perpetrated against them. The novelist describes the senseless violence of phalanx through the emptiness that Jim feels as he walks amongst the carnage. He looks on emotionlessly, and the strikers too after the violence becomes "sick, poisoned by their own anger."

Conclusion: Thus the novel *In Dubious Battle*, deals with the issue of struggle between the working class and the capitalists, and the striking agricultural migrants in California during the Great Depression. A Marxist analysis of the novel reveals the importance of collective action, class struggle and the exploitation of poor workers by the capitalists. It also throws light on the importance of ideology and propaganda, and the alienation of workers from their work and social existence under capitalism. Steinbeck criticizes the excesses of capitalism and communist ideology to exploit poor people for their own benefit. The novelist was familiar with the economic forces affecting people's lives, especially the impact of industrialisation. It was unfortunate that poor workers could not embrace the changes in technology and blamed landlords, banks and other financial institutions responsible for their sufferings. The novelist takes a balanced view point and documents what was happening without placing the blame on any individual or group. He deeply cared about poor workers, especially the migrants, and was politically active in seeking social justice to the oppressed through his works.

Works Cited:

Berry, Wendall. Another Turn of the Crank. Washington D.C.: Counterpoint. 1995. Print.

Bose, Arun. Marx on Exploitation and Inequality. Delhi: Oxford University Press, 1980. Print.

Eagleton, Terry. Ideology. Longman. London. 1994. Print.

Engels, Friedrich and Marx Karl. The Manifesto of Communist Party. 1848. <http//www.marxists.org/archive/marx/works/1848/communist -manifesto/chapter 1>.

French, Warren. Introduction. In Dubious Battle. Ellaine Steinbeck and Robert Wallsten. Eds. Steinbeck: A Life in Letters. New York: 1979. Print.

French, Warren. Introduction. In Dubious Battle. By John Steinbeck. 1936. New York: Penguin, 2006. Print.

Gerald D. Nash. The Great Depression and World War II. New York: Saint Martin's Press. 1979. Print.

Gramisci, Antonio. "The Formation of Intellectuals." Trans. Quintan Hoare and Geoffrey Nowell Smith. The Nortan Anthology of Theory and Criticism. Ed. Vincent B. Leitch. New York: Nortan, 2001. Print.

Marx, Karl and Engels Friedrich. Collected Works Volume 37. New York: International Publishers, 1998. Print.

Steinbeck, John. In Dubious Battle. New York: Penguin Books, 1992. Print.

Steinbeck, John. The Grapes of Wrath. New York: Penguin Books, 1992. Print.

Steinbeck, John. Of Mice and Men. Penguin Books (Australia), 2008.

Print.
Thomas, Peter D. The Gramscian Moment: Philosophy, Hegemony and Marxism. BRILL, 2009.

Watts, Emily Stipes. The Businessmen in American Literature. Athens, GA: University of Georgia Press, 1993. Print.
Tyson, Louis. Critical Theory Today. New York: Routledge, 2006. Prin

11. Male Consciousness in V. S. Naipaul's *A House for Mr. Biswas*

Dr Neena

Abstract: This chapter aims at discussing the male consciousness in *A House for Mr. Biswas*. The famed and well-known novel, *A House for Mr. Biswas* by V. S. Naipaul, published in 1961, has received praise from readers all over the world and is often regarded as the pinnacle work of Naipaul's memorable literary career. Naipaul satirises the socio-economic classes through Mr. Biswas' many relationships and encounters with people in diverse settings and positions. *A House for Mr. Biswas* is the tragic story of a man who exhausts himself attempting to cope with a significant shift in his culture and viewpoint. Mr. Biswas fights the Tulsi household's prevailing influences for the majority of his life in an effort to express his uniqueness. In, *A House for Mr. Biswas*, there are two main themes. One is the topic of personal and societal growth and the other is the theme of family breakdown or dissolution in the face of contemporary pressures and tendencies. It is accurate to say that Mr. Biswas represents the oppressed who have finally achieved freedom. *A House for Mr. Biswas* is undoubtedly among the best works of English fiction.

Introduction: V. S. Naipaul was born on August 17, 1932 in Trinidad, West Indies. Critics and academics view him as the spokesperson for uprooting and rootlessness. He writes novels, travel articles and essays. His works are primarily humorous satires, some of which are about politics and elections and others on the pointless existence of urban poverty. In the year 1971, he received the Booker Prize, and in 2001, he was given the Nobel

Prize in Literature. His creative output includes both fictional and non-fictional works. His novels include *Half a Life (*2001), *Magic Seeds*, *The Mystic Masseur* (1957), *The Suffrage of Elvira* (1958), *Miguel Street* (1959), *A House for Mr. Biswas* (1961), *Mr. Stone and the Knights Companion* (1963), *The Mimic Men* (1967), *A Flag on the Island* (1967), *In a Free State* (1971) which won the Booker Prize, *Guerrillas* (1975), *A Bend in the River* (1979), *The Enigma of Arrival* (2004). The Indian-born British author Naipaul is well recognized for his comedic yet biting works. It's interesting to note that Naipaul wrote *A House for Mr. Biswas* with his first wife Patricia Ann Hale in mind; sadly, Patricia passed away in 1996. Almost all of his works centre on a feeling of dislocation and alienation. For his pessimistic works, Naipaul is best known. As a former colonial who has since become homeless and global, Naipaul sees himself. He might be viewed as someone who has transferred a lot of his personal experiences of the present world into literature due to his ability to write more about himself and his past. The significant social, psychological, political, and cultural transformation of our day is exemplified by his singular experience. The book being studied is a representation of the Trinidadian East-Indian neighbourhoods where he was born and raised. The multicultural community of Trinidad has a long history of working primarily in agriculture under the indenture system. Through the migration process, they bring with them primarily rural British Indian experiences, their inherent differences, and their home cultural surroundings. Their love of their native culture and all of its ramifications are fundamental elements of who they are.

The famed and well-known novel, *A House for Mr. Biswas* by V. S. Naipaul, published in 1961, has received praise from readers all over the world and is often regarded as the pinnacle work of Naipaul's memorable literary career. It served as a milestone for his literature as well. With the publication of *A House for Mr. Biswas*, Naipaul began his major era of fiction and cemented his place among the greatest novelists of the 20th century. Since Naipaul first revealed his writing characteristics in A *House for Mr. Biswas* - his fixation with failure, exile, alienation, the search for identity, and his later harsh criticism of disadvantaged and vulnerable societies the novel represents a turning point in his literary career. In the novel, Naipaul describes the lifestyles of West Indians. Mr. Biswas is "unhomely" in this situation. The cultural exile has left him in a state of psychological limbo. Naipaul created a psychological limbo for his protagonist as a result of his alienation from his people's culture. As they themselves struggle with a divided culture, the authors of post-colonial literature tackled the notions of alienation and exile.

A House for Mr. Biswas, in various ways, brings jointly the central views of thc picaresque novel. Naipaul satirises the socioeconomic classes through Mr. Biswas' many relationships and encounters with people in diverse settings and positions. Novel is primarily realistic due to its rich scenario details. Because of the story's background of poverty, overcrowding, and instability, owning a private residence becomes the ideal objective for a resident of Trinidad, giving the work its symbolic significance. In a certain sense, the novel, *A House for Mr. Biswas* is autobiographical. *A House for Mr. Biswas* is based on Naipaul's personal experiences in Trinidad. Mr. Biswas is a representation of Seeprasad, Naipaul's father, and Anand, Mr. Biswas' son, of Naipaul. According to Naipaul, the bond between his father and him is comparable to that between Anand and Mr. Biswas, the father of Anand. For instance, Mr. Biswas and Seeprasad, Naipaul's father, both had rural birthplaces. Before having their own home, they both move into numerous different residences. Some of the commonalities include doing a variety of jobs, living with wealthy relatives, being married to thc daughters of conservative wealthy Hindu households, and painting signs. Once more, Seeprasad Naipaul discovers employment on a newspaper after relocating to Port of Spain, just like Mohun Biswas. The experiences in Mr. Biswas' son Anand's life mirror those in Naipaul's own.

A House for Mr. Biswas is the tragic story of a man who exhausts himself attempting to cope with a significant shift in his culture and viewpoint. Before the age of forty, he deems his career to be over and bases his ambitions on his children. Even if the house is jerry-built and only partially paid for or when he passes away, Mr. Biswas gained little for himself, but he leaves his children in a better position to adapt to a changing society. He is the change of first generational causality. He starts off with nothing and only accomplishes a little. The phrase "nothing will come of nothing", which he was taught to memorize early in his childhood, haunts his existence. He succeeded in creating a modest house out of nothing. Mr. Biswas had to overcome two challenges in order to go beyond what was "ought." The first is to overcome the fatalistic, passive mindset left by his ancestors and the second is to rebel against an oppressively restricted, traditional society that is itself falling apart. The belief of the kindness or indifference of fate was passed down to Mr. Biswas's family and his maternal grandfather welcomed his own birth as a proof of it:

> Bipti's father, futile with asthma, propped himself up on his string bed, and said, as he always did on unhappy occasions, 'Fate'. There is nothing we can do about it. (AHB, 13).

Mr. Biswas fights the Tulsi household's prevailing influences for the majority of his life in an effort to express his uniqueness. If, Mrs. Tulsi is the archetypal coloniser, the master, then it is obvious that the while exercise aims to colonise and subjugate. However, it is simple to romanticize Biswas' rebellious temperament and much-heralded rebellion against the conformity-subsistence/ master-slave mentality that the Tulsi family worked so painstakingly to establish and uphold. We see Biswas' epic battle against impending poverty and reliance on the Tulsi in his efforts to establish an independent household with his wife Shama. This independent, sensitive, and somewhat more educated son-in-law, who secretly harbored romantic fantasies of bravery and adventure fostered by his reading of the English Classics, finds Mrs. Tulsi's haughty dominance over that whim she protects too much. Even though it is fantasy, he is able to escape Tulsi's control thanks to it:

> The organisation of the Tulsi house was simple, Mrs. Tulsi had only one servant, a negro woman who was called Blackie by Seth and Mrs. Tulsi…Miss Blackie's duties were vague. The daughters and their children swept and washed and cooked and serve in the store. The husbands, under Seth's supervision, worked on the Tulsi land, looked after the Tulsi animals, and served in the store. In return they were given food, shelter and a little money—Mr. Biswas had no money and no position; he was expected to become a Tulsi; at once he rebelled. (AHB, 97)

In, *A House for Mr. Biswas*, there are two main themes. One is the topic of personal and societal growth, and the other is the theme of family breakdown or dissolution in the face of contemporary pressures and tendencies. The protagonist's harrowing "search for identity" is described throughout the novel. Mr. Biswas finds himself married to Shama, a member of the affluent Tulsi family residing at Hanuman House, after failing in his attempts to establish himself as either Pundit Jairam's assistant or as an assistant to Bhandat's rum business. Mr. Biswas discovers that he will have to live a life of servitude and complete submission to Mrs. Tulsi and Seth at Hanuman House. He resists against this system that requires his unquestioned devotion since he is a man of reason. Hanuman House, with its emphasis on the joint family system, in which the head of the family is the primary authority, is a symbol of traditionalism, conservation, and the old Hindu culture. The beginning of Mr. Biswas' personality development and identity search is his rebellion against this system. Hanuman House kicks Mr. Biswas out for refusing to follow the rules of behavior. To take over the Tulsi food store, he has now travelled to The Chase. He discovers that he lacks the skills necessary to run a shop and interact with clients. Mr. Biswas is forced by Shama to consent to the holding of a house blessing ceremony, despite his initial opposition. Mr. Biswas struggled to pay for the costly expense required for the house blessing ceremony. Mr. Biswas is quite unhappy with the accommodations provided at The Chase. Mr. Biswas has occasionally felt dissatisfied since he wasn't asked for his opinion on the name of his first child, who was born to him, and he also dislikes being called a laborer on the child's birth certificate. Even so, Mr. Biswas acknowledges that Hanuman House is a haven to which he is drawn fairly frequently. This demonstrates his conflicted feelings of love and hatred for Hanuman House, where he refers to the Tulsi family as 'blood suckers'. Naipaul himself and his protagonist strive to maintain their uniqueness despite becoming aware of the infantile structure of their community. In addition, Mr. Biswas and his family are given a room in the 'barracks' at Greenvale, where he feels just as uneasy as he did at Hanuman House. His suffering is caused by his unwillingness to submit to any form of regimentation.

However, he is at least relieved to be at Greenvale because he is no longer in close physical contact to the Tulsi family. Because of his desire for independence and to live in a tidy home of his own, Mr. Biswas chooses to start a house-building project. However, because he lacks the necessary funds, he cannot finish the project and instead feels frustrated. As a result, he has a nervous breakdown and needs to be brought to Hanuman House so that he can be treated before being sent back to hell. Mr. Biswas believes it would be impossible for him to continue living at Hanuman House as a Mr. Tulsi dependent once he has recovered from his sickness. In order to discover fish woods and pastures new, he departs from Hanuman House and travels to Port of Spain. Here, Mr. Biswas' shifting between locations is illustrative of his inability to pinpoint his true identity as well as of his unstable mental condition brought on by the struggle between his body, mind, and soul. In addition, his best attribute, which is his unwillingness to remain in any person's subordination, which is what, lifts him up to realize his identity. Later, after a brief stay in short hills, he travels to Port of Spain with his family and is given a few rooms in the same home where Mrs. Tulsi had previously provided housing. Mr. Biswas has no peace of mind at all because a large number of other Tulsi clan members have recently moved into this residence in Port of Spain. Mr. Biswas fights with both Mrs. Tulsi and Awad because to the hardship of living in this noisy, crowded home. When Mrs. Tusli begs him to leave her home, Mr. Biswas says he is sorry he came here on that particular day.

Mr. Biswas constructs a home in Greenvale, which the neighbourhood laborers later set on fire because they had been unfriendly toward the Tulsi family. He mocks the Tulsi family for leaving Arwacas and moving to this far-off place, proving that his yearning for independence and self-assertion is futile, but he hasn't lost his humour or his spirit. Additionally, the ashes can be gathered and utilised as a form of fertiliser. As a result, he never loses spirit despite his tragedy. Later, Mr. Biswas borrows $4 from his uncle Ajodha to purchase a new home in Port of Spain's Sikkim Street. Even if the house is later shown to have numerous flaws, Mr. Biswas has finally become the honour of a house and has fulfilled his long-cherished goal. Mr. Biswas has now reached his full potential as a human, a journalist, and a fully realised private person. His search for his identity is complete because he has now been set free from the mayhem and conundrum of his prior uncertain life. However, Mr. Biswas decides to fight back in his search for his identity, which is undoubtedly his greatest strength. According to Maurner Warner, Naipaul used Hanuman House as a "symbol of traditionalism, rigidity, culture infallibility, ceremonial duty hierarchy, and communal life." The houses stand in for Mr. Biswas' hero's resistance to buckle under the pressure of society, but in the end, he discovered a "half-lot of land, his own bit of the planet."

Conclusion: Thus, *A House for Mr. Biswas* is a fictitious novel that examines the competing ideologies and social contradictions of various classes and groups. Mr. Biswas' strong desire with forging his own personality creates an outstanding confrontation with the traditional Tulsi setup. The protagonist is motivated to battle against the lifeless, decaying rituals, myths, and practises of a corrupted Brahmin cultural system represented by the Tulsis in the story by his passion for natural human liberty and individuality. The protagonist, Mr. Biswas, has been pitted against traditional, conservative Hindu views and worldview. He is the sole opponent of the conservative system, which is rife with corrupt myths, practices and rituals and he is entirely alone in the crowd. Mr. Biswas' rebellious spirit was sparked by the underlying force of these constricting beliefs held by the Hindu community. Against the prevailing forces of dogmatism and automatic behaviour, this man stands alone. He does this in an effort to develop his own identity in society and free himself from the harsh. Thus, it can be concluded that the struggle of Mr. Biswas and sense of security is understood in precise and personal terms. It is accurate to say that Mr. Biswas represents the oppressed who have finally achieved freedom. *A House for Mr. Biswas* is undoubtedly among the best works of English fiction.

Work Cited:

Bolfarine, M., (2012). Literacy, Imagination and Autonomy in A House for Mr. Biswas. Acta Scientiarum. Language and Culture, 34 (1), 103-106.

Chinnam, V., S., (2014). Postcolonial Socio-Cultural Aspects in V. S Naipaul's A House for Mr. Biswas. International Multidisciplinary Research Journal, II (V), 82-91.

Hussein Dizayi, S., A., (2019). Postcolonial Identity Crisis in the Mimic Men a Novel by V. S. Naipaul. International Journal of Scientific Research and Management, 7(3), 920–926.

Kumar, Sanjiv, (2012). Daisporic Transformation: Novels of V. S. Naipaul. Rawat Publication, Jaipur.

Mohammed, Farman, Ullah, Bhuiyan, (2019). Diaspora Identities and Psychic Trauma in V. S. Naipaul's A House for Mr. Biswas and the Mimic Men: A Postcolonial Perspective. International Journal of English, Literature and Social Science, 4(5), 1416-1419.

Naipaul, V., S., (1961). A House for Mr. Biswas. Penguins Publishers, London.

Pandian, I., B., (2009). Life and Works of V. S. Naipaul: A Critical Study. Bhaskar Publications, Kanpur.

Singh, Bijender, (2013). Representation of Postcolonial Identity in Naipaul's Works. International Journal of English and Literature, 4(10), 451-455.

Sharma, S., K., (2016). The Struggle of Mr. Biswas Against Power and Oppression: A Study of V.S. Naipaul's A House for Mr. Biswas, Pune Research Scholar: An International Multidisciplinary Journal, 2(1).

Suma, Gilbert, (2020). Self-Exploration in A House For Mr. Biswas. Research Journal of English Language and Literature, 8 (3), 95-97.

Tas, R., M., (2011). Alienation, Naipaul and Mr. Biswas. International Journal of Humanities and Social Science, 1(11), 115-11

White, Landeg, (1975). V. S. Naipaul: A Critical Introduction. Barnes and Noble Books, New York.

12. An Eco-Feministic Framework: An Analysis of Wordsworth's *The Solitary Reaper* and *Lucy Poems*

Dr Anuradha
Dr Suneela Sharma

Abstract: Eco-feminism is an interdisciplinary theoretical movement which had its roots somewhere in 1800s but emerged at first in the United States in second half of 20th century. In its journeyof evolution, this movement went through phases of demolition and resurgence. As climate change awareness and subsequent activism rose in recent decades, feminists began to identifysimilarity between the demand for gender equality and protection of environment. This led to a struggle against the prioritization of development at the cost of nature in sync with the discrimination against women. The plundered womb of earth for the sake of commercialvested human greed came to be identified with the subjugation of women by the patriarchal societal norms.
Eco-feminism disseminated by, Francoise d' Eaubonne in 1970s, is a kind of philosophy which confers the essential issues of ecosystem and feminism. Heather Eaton and Lois Ann Lorentzen, in Ecofeminism and Globalization, say: "Ecofeminism encompasses a variety of theoretical, practical, and critical efforts to understand and resist the interrelated dominations of women and nature" (1). Eco-feminism thus brings together fundamentals of green movements and feminism under a systemic phenomenon. According to this, the relationship between nature and women is

very identical, strong and powerful. It is identical in their constitution as both, woman and nature, in their essence, symbolise innocence and purity. The invasion or destruction of nature through pollution and materialistic gains is very close to the violation of the chastity of a girl child in its philosophical and metaphorical interpretation. To preserve the purity or richness of nature and the chastity or self-respect of women is, therefore an identical agenda present in the Eco-feminism. Romanticism emerged as an artistic movement which influenced writers to express their emotions simply and freely. William Wordsworth, the foremost poet of the Romantic age who worshiped nature in his poems, knowingly or unknowingly adhered to the concept of Eco-feminism. His women characters reflect the over-powering innocence, virtue and optimism of nature. Wordsworth believes that nature is self-sufficient in its own abundance. He enlightens people about the love of nature through *The Solitary Reaper* and *Lucy Poems*. He conveys an intense concern for the purity of nature in "The Solitary Reaper and devotes himself as a worshipper of nature. Nature is as a teacher and guide to him in the Lucy Poems. Thus, his poetry reflects nature in her grandeur and reduces human ego to a humble submission before nature. The harmony between women and nature in his poems has created curiosity of researchers to study his poems under eco-feministic framework. This different mood helps critics to investigate Wordsworth's works as they find his poems full of sensibility, spirituality, intimate consciousness of natural things, and independent work (Bloom 174-175). Nature affects the activities of women and Wordsworth is a feminist who, through "The Solitary Reaper" and Lucy Poems presents pastoral image of the society.

One of the most beautiful poems which fall under the eco-feministic framework is "The Solitary Reaper". The poem, written in 1805, and published in 1807 in the collection Poems, in Two Volumes, is in eco-feministic framework as it reflects the beauty of landscape and the reaper who is single in the field and singing an unknown tune. She seems quite close to nature. Sherry Onter in his essay "Is Female to Male as Nature is to Culture" says, "Eco- feminists argue that cross-culturally and historically women as opposed to men, have been seen as close to nature because of their physiological nature, social role and psychology (67-68).

William Wordsworth projects the solitary reaper as a submissive reaper who is unaffected by the surroundings or passers-by. She is busy in her reaping and the poet assumes that she is singing a sad song. She lives in a natural world and for her nature is everything. The poet directs passers-by not to disturb the Highland lass as she is singing a melodious song. They should either stop and behold her utmost purity or gently pass so that she may not be distracted. The whole valley echoes solitary reaper's song and is overflowing with the beautiful sound.

> Behold her, single in the field,
> Yon solitary Highland Lass!
> Reaping and singing by herself;
> Stop here, or gently pass!
> Alone she cuts and binds the grain,
> And sings a melancholy strain;
> O listen! for the Vale profound
> Is overflowing with the sound.

Wordsworth praises the girl and compares her song to nightingale and cuckoo bird; here also we can see eco- feministic framework as the reaper is compared with birds. She is singing more melodiously than these two birds and helping the travellers to tranquil. The reaper's song is a confluence of such conflicting sentiments- reinforcement, comfort in loneliness and anticipation in hostile settings. Wordsworth is also affected by the song and feels comfortable. Though the song is melancholic yet the expressions signify to be empowering the freedom of expression of the rural woman. Sally Baker depicts, If the text is interpreted through the lens of gender performativity theory, the solitary reaper is 'not only embodied through the poet speaker's relation to the feminine, but also through the speaker's literal analysis of her song' (5). The critic further asserts that Wordsworth's interpretation of the song is entirely rooted in his individual 'musical knowledge' (5). The expression "stop here or gently pass", speak volumes about the undaunted devotion of the poet towards nature as he almost orders any passer-by not to disturb the solitary woman who is reaping and singing by herself. The reaper and the valley echoing the melodious song are identical to the poet in their respective ideal forms of solitariness. He leaves no choice to a passer-by other than letting the song; the reaper and the beautiful valley co-exist in their unblemished undisturbed status. Words such as behold, alone, single, solitary, all by herself, gently pass, profound and overflowing create an intense chemistry between the solitary reaper and the abundant nature around her that seems to breathe around the reaper in full life.

> No Nightingale did ever chant
> More welcome notes to weary bands
> Of travellers in some shady haunt,
> Among Arabian sands:
> A voice so thrilling ne'er was heard
> In spring-time from the Cuckoo-bird,
> Breaking the silence of the seas
> Among the farthest Hebrides.

The comforting sweetness and the quality of freshness in the song of the solitary reaper is depicted by the use of pectoral metaphors of nightingales and cuckoos in the second stanza. Phrases like "Arabian sands", "the silence of the seas" and "the Farthest Hebrides" carry us far and wide in search for a better quality of song than that of the solitary reaper but at the same time a brilliant imagery is used by the poet to draw parallels between the woman and the female birds, thereby exploring the layers of eco-feminism.

The birds comfort the wearybands of travellers in Arabian desert or the farthest islands of Hebrides while the lonely reaper fills the valley with her profound song and mesmerises the tired traveller.

Will no one tell me what she sings?
Perhaps the plaintive numbers flow
For old, unhappy, far-off things,
And battles long ago:
Or is it some more humble lay,
Familiar matter of to-day?
Some natural sorrow, loss, or pain,
That has been, and may be again?

Wordsworth is not able to understand what the Highland girl is singing as she is singing in her local dialect yet he appreciates its tone, its expressive beauty, and the feeling it gives to him. It is, however, notable that he just makes lame excuse that she might be singing of her sorrows, pain or losses she has suffered in past or battles fought long ago. He even guesses that her song may be about some suffering that may be recurring in her everyday life. Here, one's imagination is inadvertently drawn towards the physiological role of a country woman as the worker in fields and of a mother, a domestic household worker at home. Herstereotype as a supressed silent worker who cannot or even does not question this role. At thesame time we identify this reaper with the silent nature who is her friend and confidant, her silent witness as well as her echoing audience. There is a silent undertone of sadness in these lines.

Whate'er the theme, the Maiden sang
As if her song could have no ending;
I saw her singing at her work,
And o'er the sickle bending;
I listened, motionless and still;

And, as I mounted up the hill,
The music in my heart I bore,
Long after it was heard no more.

The fact the poet has not understood the meaning of the song is so fascinating that the readers too turn thoughtful and reflexive consciousness helps the writer to bear the song in his heart. This song has given him so much joy that he carries this song in his heart and finds peace and solace after recollecting it in his mind the hones of tranquillity. Thus in *The Solitary Reaper* the poet reflects a relationship of harmony between the nature and the feministic experience.

Lucy Poems is a series of five poems first printed in Lyrical Ballads in 1800. Lucy in these poems is a mysterious female figure whose intimacy with nature is unparalleled. WilliamWordsworth depicts her as a nature's child. He personifies nature in his Lucy poems and says, "Three years she grew in sun and shower". Nature nurtures Lucy to grow amidst all kinds of weather be it sun or rain in order to mature her not in years but in experience and wisdom. Nature cultivates her as "sportive as a fawn" who carries a quiet grace even in the stormiest of emotional circumstances. She is in ecological framework that needs sun and water to grow and imbibe the quality of feminine grace and gait from such a beautiful and graceful animal as a fawn. Alex Jackson says, "Wordsworth's series is as much as ecological endeavour as it is love or mourning" (8). In the first poem "Strange fits of passion I have known" Wordsworth recollects his journey towards Lucy's cottage during the evening and the moon sinks lower throughout the journey. The poet is disappointed by a sudden disappearance of the moon which was a guiding light for him. Wordsworth describes her as a beautiful and solitary maiden and says "She dwelt among the untrodden ways", the untrodden signifying her innocence. Her existence on earth was short. Though she was isolated and has never met anyone in this world yet she has left an indelible mark on the poet. He is haunted by her absence now that she is dead. Death of Lucy is identical to the loss of nature's purity and the poet seems to lament for both when he laments for Lucy's death. Later, in the series, he claims "I travelled among unknown men" and reflects upon visiting foreign lands outside of England and how it took being away from his homeland to make him fully appreciate the natural beauty. He contemplates the loss of Lucy to early death and falls in depths of emotions. In "A slumber did my spirit seal", the poet succumbs to realities of mortality and becomes totally drained of the power to feel anything in light of his overwhelming loss. However, the solace is that she does not die and continues to live in the framework of time and space. He presents Lucy here as a cosmic body that can hear what others cannot say. Alex Jackson says, "The Lucy poems play to the epistemological uncertainty ...collapsingsuch a division to give equal weight to the non-human voice". (6)

Conclusion: *The Solitary Reaper* and *Lucy Poems* of William Wordsworth have feminized nature in various facets. He has symbolically articulated women as part of nature in both the poems and portrayed its relation with nature. These poems reflect restoration, renovation, reformation and self-renewal in terms of femininity. Carolyn Merchant reveals in The Death of Nature - our mind determines our behaviour, the way we consider nature determines the wayhow we treat nature. Merchant's remarks that the metaphor of feminized nature affects and regulates human's attitude to the earth could be applied in literary interpretation. Thus Wordsworth's poems inspire and instigate researchers to explore the interplay of nature and women as complements to each other, together and similar in their experiences, playing central role in his poetry.

Works Cited

Jackson, Alex. "Reading Lucy, Rereading Nature: An Ecological Approach to Wordsworth's Lucy Poems". SFU Library Digital Publishing , 2017. PP(5-8)

Baker, Sally. "The Projection of Performativity: A Theoretical Feminist Approach to William
Wordsworth's "The Solitary Reaper". UA Library 2015. www.undergraduatelibrary.org/2015/literature-1710-present/projection-performativity-theoretical-feminist-approach-william. Accessed 2 July 2017.
Onter, Sherry. "Is Female to Male as Nature is to Culture?" Woman, Culture, and Society, Stanford University Press, 1974, PP 67-68.
Eaton, Heather, and Lois Ann Lorentzen. Ecofeminism and Globalization: Exploring Culture, Context, and Religion. Littlefield Publishers, 2003.
Merchant, Carolyn. The Death of Nature: Women, Ecology, and the Scientific Revolution.
Harper San Francisco, 1980.
Stork, Charles. "The Influence of the Popular Ballad on Wordsworth and Coleridge":
William Wordsworth, edited by. Harold Bloom. Yale UP, 1914.

13. *The Mahabharata*: Relevance In Contemporary India

Anuradha
Dr Atul Rasika Moudgil

Abstract: The *Mahabharata*, a long narrative text written in Sanskrit and penned down around 400 B.C. to 400 C.E. by Maharishi Ved Vyasa, is perhaps one of the greatest epics ever written and carried from generation to another in our country through both oral and written means. Though written long back, this epic becomes significant as well as relevant in the present times through its universal moral teachings and values especially propounded by Lord Krishna during the battle of *Mahabharata*. The story revolves around the Pandavas, who were the incarnations of their fathers (gods), and the Kauravas (their cousins), who were ever indulged in the corrupt politics and war tactics. Dharma and Karma are the concepts entwined in the great treatise of the *Mahabharata*. The values and virtues such as non-violence, peace, unconditional love, right way of thinking etc are conceived as central to human conduct and ideal way of living,

Key-words: society, dharma, karma, culture, women oppression and caste discrimination.

> yadâ yadâ hi dharmasya glânir bhavati bhârata
> abhyutthânam adharmasya tadâtmânaA s [ijâmyaham
> Chapter 4: Jñâna Karma Sanyâs Yog, Verse 7

Maharishi Ved Vyasa is known as one of the greatest and legendary sages of Hindu religion. According to Hindu scriptures, there were

28 Vyasas. In the long run of Dvapara Yuga, the enlightened, venerable and eminent Maharishi Ved Vyasa was born around the third millennium. The birth name of Ved Vyasa was Krishna Dvaipayana (referring to his complexion and place of birth). He is better known as Ved Vyasa that means 'the one who classified the vedas'. These four Vedas are (I) Rig Veda (II) Samaveda (III) Yajurveda (IV) Atharveda. He is also referred to as the Guru of Dattatreya, who is memorized as 'Guru of Gurus'. He is also the word-smith as well as a cast in one of the greatest Hindu epics the *Mahabharata*.

Numerous epithets have been devoted to the *Mahabharata*, sometimes called 'Itihasa', sometimes 'Purana' and sometimes 'Kavya' which show its multi-dimensional aspect but putting it in the category of mythology, chronicles or legends would be a crime to its richness. It is approximately seven times the length of the Odyssey and Iliad together, and 15 times the length of the Bible. The *Mahabharata* is a long narrative text in Sanskrit and contains eighteen books. The title 'Maha' indicates the size of the text and 'Bharat' denotes two sets of cousins. It has neither a single hero nor a single author. It tells the story of the five Pandava brothers and one hundred Kaurva brothers. It highlights their lives before, during, and after the battle at Kurukshetra. On the surface level, war was over the kinship of their ancestral realm. The epic draws special attention to Pandavas from birth, childhood, and life after marriage to Draupadi till their deaths. This Pandava narrative is not told at a fixed rate and style. It is adjourned and jazzed up along the way by many sub-stories and variegated teachings which characters tell to each other and to readers inside the text. The often called 'Upakhyanas' i.e., sub-stories is the indispensable facet of the *Mahabharata*. In every case, the chronicle is formally conferred as an influential correspondencc between the teller and the told, which may conciliate repeatedly to direct the teller or to ask for details that mark the *Mahabharata* an intriguing text to inquire into and decipher it.

In broaden term, concerning principles of the *Mahabharata* are problems and possibilities of governance mostly open at the level of society. The society especially settles around the figure of the king. The range of the *Mahabharata* goes beyond the human and falls into the cosmic level. Evidently, it is a narrative of a battle, even after the sanctities there is so much left that we can metaphorically establish a link with ultra-modern civilization. The *Mahabharata* through its narrative teaches the rule of law to the society. The epic is reminiscence of dharma. There is divinity, ethereality, and transmundanity in it. First and foremost, dharma is about one's secluded choice. As Dr Bibek Debroy reiterates:

> It is not the society which is telling you what to do, it is not the king who is telling you what to do, and it is your own individual decision. And that is the most important message of the *Mahabharata*. Depending on the individual decision you take, depending on what you perceive to be dharma, you will have to face the consequences. (13)

Religion is not something one adopts today and gives up tomorrow. It is something perennial. It is primeval. It is a code of conduct that consists of certain principles and these laws/ ideas and principles are valid for every age and it has a universal appeal. These are fundamental and conceived as central to human perfection. It sets some standards on which people and their actions are being judged. One is struck by the pervasive impact this creation has on the life of an average Indian. In a sense, the *Mahabharata* is like any other piece of fictional work that contains "a set of human agents" (Jhanji 4) and a storyline. But if we examine this work through "purânic tradition" (Jhanji 4) lens, it is rich in allegories and philosophy, and putting all these elements together creates a phenomenal world picture. As to Ralph Waldo Emerson states:

> I owed a magnificent day to the Bhagavad-Gita. It was as if an empire spoke to us, nothing small

or unworthy, but large, serene, consistent, the voice of an old intelligence which in another age and climate had pondered and thus disposed of the same questions which exercise us.

According to Mircea Eliade says, "We become really human when we have followed the learning of the myths, imitated the gods" (11). We find it interesting how it could be possible that such age-old writing aptly covers various modern age social and moral issues. This writing challenges our cognitive ability. There is an ocean of endless questions but we manage to collect some drops of it. Let us discuss some of the important and relevant points which are not only connected to one of the greatest epics of India but also concerned to the modern age.

1) Hasn't Forgiveness become a necessary trait in the present day?
2) Doesn't the epic teach about Truth and Right Living?
3) Isn't greed the start of downfall?
4) Aren't women still subjected to humiliation?
5) Isn't virginity the only parameter of chastity?
6) Aren't people spreading scandals about unwed mothers?
7) Isn't a woman considered a whore for having more than one sexual partner?
8) Internalizing the caste prejudice.
9) Isn't there any shrewd politician like Sri Krishna?
10) Isn't a woman struggling to wipe the tag of property?
11) Aren't couples visiting sperm banks to get impregnated?
12) Aren't we using the lesson of non-violence?
13) Is a woman's honour cheaper than one's word?

The paramount certitude of the world as suggested by the 'Gita' is that all creatures on earth are souls bound by the mortal bodies

(Jivatma). As Shri Krishna in chapter 2, Verse 20 says, "na jâyate mriyate vâ kadâchin nâyaAbhûtvâ bhavitâ vâ na bhûya% ajo nitya% úhâúhvato is A purâGona hanyate hanyamâne úharîre" (English Translation Of Sri Shankaracharya is Sanskrit Commentary By Swami Gambirananda). The transfiguration through birth, development, maturity and death is only of the body, not of the self. A soul (atman) cannot be created or obliterated. The only course of action for salvation is consistent righteousness of thought or to be thoughtless, right speech and execution of the right deed.

It is the harsh truth that the condition of women was not much privileged even though people at that point in time had chosen to remain tight-lipped. Draupadi, the wife of the Pandavas, was lost at a venture in a bet to Dhritrashtra. Draupadi delineated one of the most powerful speeches where she asserts that nobody can claim her own without her accede. In the middle of the royal assembly Dushasana drags her. In a state of indignation Draupadi takes an oath that she will not tie her locks until she douses it with Dushasana's blood. She takes the place of a bloodthirsty woman who knows how to be on one's feet. It speaks the fact that if any man touches a woman without her consent; he will have to get the grips with the repercussion, and will never be acquitted. All persons should know their extremities and never dare to exceed them. The consequence of Kauravas' misdeed becomes the lead example. It will be apt to say,

> "yatra nâryastu pûjyante ramante tatra devatâ
> yatraitâstu na pûjyante sarvâstatrâphalâ: kriyâ:e

According to the *Mahabharata* tale, Amba was the eldest daughter of Kashya. Along with her sisters Ambika and Ambalika, she was abducted by Bhishma from their Swayamvara. (He provoked the assembled Kings and Princes and defeated them.) He presented them to Satyavati (mother) for marriage to Vichitravirya (his brother), the crowned head of Hastinapura. Amba had already given her heart to another man, Vichitravirya but he married only her sisters and rejected her. When she went back to her beloved, he rejected her in ignomity of losing the fight against Ganga-putra at the Swayamvara. Amba then came back to Ganga-putra and laid claim that he should tie wedlock with her. Since he had already got a hitch to bachelorhood he turned down her condition. Amba got antagonized on the fact that she would remain an unmarried woman, and she blasphemed to kill him, at least in her next life, and then lost his life. She was reborn as Shikhandi to king Drupad. In the battle of Kurukshetra, she fulfilled her desire and became one and the only instrument of Bhishma's death.

Kunti, the mother of Pandavas, was granted the boon to bring forth a child with pertinent divine qualities from the gods by rishi Durvasha. Kunti, to test his blessing, evoked the god of Sun and as a result Karna was born to an unmarried Kunti inconspicuous. She stood in awe of outrage and kickback from society over her adulterated pregnancy, Kunti left with no choice but to turn her back on the newly born baby and adrift him in a basket on the holy Ganges River in the daydream that he would encounter his parents. Karna was discovered and taken care of by his foster parents. But the unfortunate Kunti was neither in the state to celebrate the birth of her son nor to mourn his death.

Yudhishthira, who had been invited and tricked by Duryodhana in a game of chess, lost all his possessions along with his wife Draupadi and his brothers. On this, Draupadi invokes shastras,and challenging that not a husband, father, nor even the gods, no one has the right to bet a woman. Hearing this Karna calls Draupadi a "whore" for marrying five men and directs Dushasana to take off her saree. Through Draupadi had five husbands but at that moment, they were so helpless that no one could defend on the height of her insult. It was not only that Karna his took revenge for being called a 'Shurda' but by provoked Dushana to do so he also satisfied his male ego. The same is happening around us when a girl rejects a boy and falls victim either to 'rape' or 'acid attack' in the present day.

This is being expected from a woman to walk along with her husband even if he deserves it or not. The same happened to Draupadi and it is still applicable on women. After marrying, Arjuna, Draupadi had gone through a lot. Being a wife, it was her duty to serve her husbands even in adversities. First, she was forced to live like an average woman even being a queen. On losing her in gambling, she argues that no one has the right to bet a woman. When exile of 12 years followed by a year of Agyatavasa, meaning "living incognito", Yudhishtira again accepts the invitation of gambling and loses, and goes into exile with his brothers and wife Draupadi. In modern times, a wife is still struggling to get her rights, will and liberty because what we understand the word 'wife' is a well-trained and sophisticated husband maid.

Many a times, Draupadi was criticized for marrying five men. Whereas, Pandu was the king of the Kuru kingdom, he was married to Kunti and Madri. Men are never judged by society. When he went hunting in the woods he saw a couple of deer during their intercourse, and shot arrows at them. Then Sage Kindama cursed Pandu with the inability of having children and he informed his wives that with the intent of making love he would be cursed to die. After that Kunti evoked her blessing with the prior permission of Pandu to have children with the power of different gods. And thus Pandu had five children Yudhishthiras by Dharmaraja, Bhima by Vayu, Arjuna by Indra, Nakula, and Sahadeva by Ashvins.

Krishna was the virtuous designer of the *Mahabharata* who had already knew all the possible of the "aryavarta" right from Gandhara to Manipura and Himalayas to Dandakaranya, its politics, physical geography as well as economics. Notwithstanding the laws, Krishna was all about dhrama (duty/righteousness). He fought against the unprincipled, fraudulent, and villainous agent of politics but he resorted to unethical politics. He pleads the king Dhristrashtra to avoid war by giving Pandavas their due inheritance. Krishna's disgraceful entry and his valuable advice are offset by the foolish king. Duryodhna with his malafied intension makes the mistake of arresting and humiliating Krishna (who has come only to make entreaty for peace as an envoy), and has to pay by losing everything, even his and his dear ones' lives. He said that there should be governing ethos to a certain extent.

The epic helps to imbibe the superior values of life in the generations to come. As the warring factions of the Kauravas and the Pandavas are prepared for the battle at Kurukshetra, the latter (Pandavas) endeavours for the last call for peace and non-violence by sending their dearest Krishna as their 'Dut' (envoy) to Kaurava court. Krishna pleads the king Dhritarashtra to avoid war by giving Pandavas their due inheritance. Krishna's graceful entry and his valuable advice are offset by the foolish king. Later we are informed that Duryodhna has to pay back by losing everything even his clan. The epic makes the relevance of non-violence and morality in human life with its universal significance in every age. As we all know that during the struggle for Indian independence many well-known politicians had used the weapon of non-violence and it is still prevalent in the world.

When Draupadi came after her marriage for the first time and Arjun wanted to show this surprise to his mother, Kunti unknowingly told them "I can't come right now or the food will burn. But as always, whatever you brought should be shared equally amongst all my sons." Draupadi had cold feet but was unable to reciprocate. She wanted Arjuna to stand up for her. From ages women expect that one man stands and speaks for her. Women are always being taught that they should always seek male support even if they are capable of to take their own stand.

The *Mahabharata* plays the world of class and caste, where genealogy ascertains identity. Being the firstborn, Karna was the eldest Pandava by blood whom Kunti kept in a basket and put down in a river. A low-caste infertile couple finds the abandoned new-born and looks after him as their own child. The core questions remain unanswered what fixes a person's identity? Can an individual change or reject who he really is? Who gets to say who each of us really is? Can we cheat on our destinies? Another example is Ekalavya who had built a statue of Guru Dronacharya because he refused to accept him as a disciple, but when Ekalavya becomes the world's best archer, Drona asks him for his thumb as Guru Diksha and Ekalavya cuts off his thumb to offer it to his Guru. Here Drona ensures that Arjuna will be the best archer in the world. Shashikant Hingonekar describes this discrimination beautifully through his poem:

> If you had kept your thumb
> history would have happened
> somewhat differently.
> But ... you gave your thumb
> and history also
> became theirs.
> Ekalavya, since that day they have not even given you a glance.
> Forgive me, Ekalavya, I won't be fooled now by their sweet words.
> My thumb will never be broken. (qut. in Dalit History Month)

No doubt, we are living in twenty-first century where Artificial Intelligence and high class technology are in current but even then handful people are still living in class and caste prejudices. From the *Mahabharata* Karna and Ekalavya both is the well-known name that faced this caste and class discrimination.

It is deeply felt nowadays that in order to counter the materialistic influence of modern technology and advancement of westernization we are direly required to establish in the heart of our younger generation certain time-tested human values. In the modern age, we are surrounded by and filled with hatred, revenge and lack of love. The satisfaction of the materialistic achievement seems to be out of the table in present times. It is true that to forgive and to forget are no easy tasks to practice in life. Almost every character in the *Mahabharata* falls for this. When Karna was called 'Shudra' by Draupadi and Draupadi was addressed as 'whore' by Karna later became one of the causes for commencing war at Kurukshetra. Even today, such situations arise whether talking on a local or global level. So a change is needed not only in the behaviour of mankind, but also in the patterns of thinking in the first place.

A host of characters like Rishi Ved Vyasa, Lord Krishna, Bhishma, Draupadi, Karna, Acharyas, Pandavas, and many others served as role models to inspire for living a noble life in ancient as well as in modern times. That is why we have the tradition of oral discourses on Ramayana, Bhagvata, *Mahabharata*, Upnishadas, Bhagavad-Gita and others popular and sacred books even to this day all over India. No doubts, the time is evolving but the human nature remains the same. So the relevance of the *Mahabharata* still persists. People even today are struck with problems of clan, caste, honor, plight of the women, unethical practices in the profession, and so many other inhumane activities but the time tested values of the *Mahabharata* will always guide us and enlighten our path with motto 'yogesth kuru ḳarmani' and Vasudev Kutumbhkam.

Works Cited:

Divakaruni, Chitra B. The Palace of Illusions: A Novel. New York: Doubleday, 2008.

Emerson, Ralph . "Ralph Waldo Emerson Quote - Lib Quotes." Lib Quotes.Com, 1 Dec. 1848, quotepark.com/quotes/1830250-ralph-waldo-emerson-i-owed-a-magnificent-day-to-the-bhagavad-gita-it/ . Accessed 15 Jan. 2023.

Hingonekar, Shashikant. https://velivada.com/2017/04/27/dalit-history-month-eklavya-adivasi-dalit-rejection-brahminism/. Accessed 24 December 2022.

Jhanji, Rekha. Human Condition in the Mahabharata. Elegant Printers,

1995.
Mishra, Vijay. The Gothic Sublime. SUNY Press, 1994.
Mukundananda Swami. Bhagavad Gita:The Song of God. www.holy-bhagavad-gita.org/chapter/4/verse/7. Accessed 15 January 2023.
Narayanswamy,Ramnath.The significance of the Mahabharathahttps://www.deccanherald.com/content/373967/significance-mahabharatha.html. Accessed 10 January 2023.
Pallathadka, Harikumar, and Kirana Pallathadka, Laxmi . "INDIA THROUGH MAHABHARATA: A CRITICAL VIEW." European Journal of Molecular & Clinical Medicin, vol. Volume 07,, no. Issue 11, 2020, 2022, pp. 8257-8262, https://www.researchgate.net/publication/351871240_INDIA_THROUGH_MAHABHARATA_A_CRITICAL_VIEW. Accessed 8 Jan. 2023.
Rajagopalachari, C. Mahabharata / [tr. and adapted] by C. Rajagopalachari .Hindustan Times New Delhi ,1950.
Truschke,Audrey .The Living Mahabharata.aeon.co/essays/the-indian-epic-mahabharata-imparts-a-dark-nuanced-moral-vision. Accessed 5 January 2023.
Jha, Ganganatha. Manusmriti with the Commentary of Medhatithi.www.wisdomlib.org/hinduism/book/manusmriti-with-the-commentary-of-medhatithi/d/doc199834.html. Accessed 28 December 2022.
Bharat temple.www.bharattemples.com/bhagavad-gita-chapter-2-verse-20. Accessed 2 January 2023.

14. Toni Morrison's Strategic Use of a Distinct Narrative Technique, Myth, and Folklore for Re-Writing History of Africa in *Tar Baby*: A Narratological Study of the Novel

Dr. Balwan Singh

Abstract: The aim of this Research paper is to study Toni Morrison's strategic use of a distinct Narrative technique, Myth, and Folklore for the re-writing history of Africa in *Tar Baby*. Morrison uses myth and folklore in her writings to retell the stories as they were, but to use them as a strategy of highlighting the contemporary realities; modern comforts of city life, and the wiped-out culture and history of her ancestral Africa. She consciously and strategically uses the African-American myth of the flying Negro and folklore like the tale of Br'er Rabbit in *Tar Baby*. The change in the point of view, following shifts in the reader's perspective on characters and events, gives a high degree of concentration and intensity to the novel. In this novel, her major characters have an opportunity to present their particular views on themselves and others. And while there is an omniscient narrator, he is not given a role superior to that of each of the others. He only highlights and not prescribes or define the thoughts and actions of significant characters. Such a narrative technique definitely offers a more objective picture and a balanced narrative as is the case in *Tar Baby*.

Keywords: Narrative technique, narratology, omniscient narrator, myth and Folklore, African History

Narrative technique and Narratology are integral parts of a narrative. Narratology is the overall study of a narrative and narrative techniques are the tools through which a writer tells a story. An author uses different narrative techniques and tools to press upon her/his idea of presenting the story. Mythology, Folklore and a different style are one of the tools which help the author to tell his/her stories in a very effective way. Literary authors don't fit in myth and folklore in their writings to retell the stories as they were but to use them as a strategy of highlighting contemporary realities. Myths and oral traditions enable a writer to develop the theme, shape the structure of his/her works and represent the characters. Writers like T.S. Eliot, Girish Karnad, Alice Walker, and of course, Toni Morrison has brilliantly deployed myths and folklore in their writings. Any discussion of the novelistic or narrative technique would be meaningless if it is not related to the subject matter of the novel. "For, obviously the object of technique is to help realize the artistic intention, and we shall see over and over again how the specific effect sought by the artist determines the technical methods consciously or unconsciously chosen." (Warren, The Twentieth Century Novel: Studies in Technique, 3) After all, the technique is only a means, not an end in itself.

Toni Morrison's deployment of myth and folklore can be traced in almost every novel of Morrison including The Bluest Eye, Sula, Song of Solomon, Beloved and *Tar Baby*. She is one among others who consciously and strategically uses the African-American myth of the flying negro and folklore like the tale of Br'er Rabbit along with other folk forms like jazz music.

Morrison has incorporated myth and folklore in *Tar Baby* as a strategy for challenging the convention of omniscient point of view in literature and to promote the idea of Afrocentrism. The story of *Tar Baby* (1981) is from the children's stories about Br'er Rabbit and Br'er Bear, a folktale written by Joel Chandler Harris, a white American writer. Morrison wrote *Tar Baby* by using the version she heard as a child. In the version adopted by Morrison, there is a white farmer who makes a tar baby out of a mixture of tar and turpentine. He creates the figure to get rid of an annoying rabbit that has caused damage in his garden. The farmer dresses the tar baby in a skirt and hat and sets it in the garden to trap the rabbit. When Br'er Rabbit sees the tar baby, he comes close and says "Good Morning," hoping to hear a friendly reply. When the tar baby does not respond, the rabbit gets angry and hits the figure. Unfortunately, the rabbit gets struck in the tar. When the farmer sees Br'er Rabbit in the tar, the rabbit tries to fool the farmer with a rhyme. "Boil me in oil, skin me alive, but please do not throw me in that Briar Patch! Not knowing the rhyme is a trick, the farmer throws the rabbit into the briar patch. The rabbit manages to escape, saying to the farmer, "This is where I was born and bred at!" (Rhodes 68-69). The African slaves used the wit of this tale to escape from the cruelty of their white masters. In Morrison's *Tar Baby*, the Black servant Gideon employs this strategy. Gideon never reveals his ability to read instructions in order to escape the burden of overwork. He calmly accepts Sydney's superiority over him and never minds whenever Sydney calls him by the name 'Yardman' instead of calling him by his real name, as the identity of a black lies in his real name which consciously be wiped out by the whites. On asked why she used this story; Morrison says in an Interview:

> I use that old story because, despite its funny, happy ending, it used to frighten me. The story has a tar baby in it which is used by a white man to catch a rabbit. "*Tar Baby*" is also a name, like nigger, that white people call black children, black girls, as I recall.... I found that there is a tar lady in African mythology....At one time, a tar pit was a holy place... held together things like Moses's little boat and the pyramids. For me, the tar baby came to mean the black woman who could hold things together. The story was a point of departure

to history and prophecy. (LeClair 35)

From the Narratological prospects the very first distinction between plot and story is not immediately apparent in the way the events in the novel are related to the readers. The story in the background is set on a small fictitious island in the Caribbean, Isle des Chevaliers, named after a group of mythical African horsemen. According to the legend, the Africans were brought to the island as slaves, but they escaped and were said to be roaming the hills on horseback. Against this mythical backdrop, Morrison tells a modern love story; the story of Jadine Childs and Son Green's relationship with each other.

Morrison puts herself in a situation while dealing with the theme of the novel. On one hand, she wants to affirm the freedom of a black woman who makes choices for her own life; on the other hand, she wants to narrate the quest of the contemporary black female heroine when she happens to be a cultural orphan, one whose sense of self is based upon a denial of her cultural heritage and an identification with one that is not her own. When one tries to interpret this novel in the folkloristic pattern of interaction, it is usually interpreted as Jadine and Son as tar babies. In an interview with Nellie McKay, Morrison says:

Many of the problems modern couples have been caused not so much by conflicting gender roles as by the other differences the culture offers. Jadine and Son had no problems as far as men and women were concerned. They knew exactly what to do. But they had a problem with what to do, when and where to do it, and where to live. These things hinged on what they felt about who they were, and what their responsibilities were in being black. (13)

On one level *Tar Baby* appears to be simply the story of a failed love affair between a man and a woman with diametrically opposed values and lifestyles. On a deeper level, the novel is about the disparity Morrison sees between the women of her remembered past and the women of the present epitomized in the character of

Jadine. Consequently, the biblical epigraph to the novel makes it clear to some extent. See the following:

> For it hath been declared
> Unto me of you, my brethren, by them
> Which are of the house of
> Chloe, that there are
> Contentions among you. (Morrison, *Tar Baby*, ii)

It does not simply foretell the conflicts that arise in the Valerian Street household. Instead, it points to the serious conflicts that Morrison (born Chloe) examines in the character of Jadine. Indeed, the text reveals the dilemma Morrison faced in trying to depict the potential penalty of success predicated upon disconnection from one's racial identity and cultural heritage. *Tar Baby* is perhaps the first novel in which one can register W.E.B. Du Bois's sense of the double consciousness of African-Americans. She has identified Jadine as a woman who has forgotten her ancient properties. The phrase "ancient properties"-first appeared prior to the novel's first page. Morrison dedicated her novel to–Mrs. Caroline Smith/Mrs. Millie MacTeer/Mrs. Ardelia Willis/Mrs. Ramah Wofford/Mrs. Lois Brooks/-and each of their sisters, /all of whom knew/their true and ancient properties.

Morrison indirectly includes herself as one of those sisters the one who has remained true to her identity as an African-American woman. Morrison was in dilemma while writing *Tar Baby* as she herself had to come out of the difficulty with her identity as Toni Morrison from Chloe Wofford. Later in 1992, she identified herself: "I am really Chloe Anthony Wofford.... I have been writing under this other person's name." (Bigsy 28)

In *Tar Baby*, Morrison has attempted two new narrative strategies–situating the central plot within a limited setting beyond the geographical boundaries of the United States mainland and juxtaposing black and white characters to dramatize the racial complexities that decide the American cultural landscape. The earlier narratives are set in generally realistic American locales; a lush, exotic Caribbean Island, fully owned by one of the main characters, a retired white businessman. The central characters of Morrison's earlier novels ordinarily seek to escape the folk culture and post-slave culture origins, but most of the principal black characters in this novel appear to have succeeded in doing this. In addition, the novel employs nonsequential narration and impressionistic scene depiction. The Surrealistic, symbolic narrative here is unique to this writer's work. The emphasis on an animated nature and the presence of ghosts and spirits prepares Morrison's audience for her masterpiece, Beloved.

In comparison with Beloved, The Bluest Eye, and Jazz, *Tar Baby* is the most experimental novel of Morrison. This novel is marked by subtle and important changes in the points of view, chapter one starts with the third-person narrator interspersed with the first-person as the dialogues of the characters themselves depict the incidents of their past life. Here the narrator first describes in epic detail the transformation of Isle de Chevaliers from a natural paradise into a ravaged colonial habitat. The omniscient narrator stresses that while nature can be injured, it cannot be eliminated. Then the narrator moves the focus to a single house, Valerian's L'Arbe de la Croix, which is described as a comforting place. The narrator explains that Valerian has moved away from his native Philadelphia and has chosen both to retire and to consider himself an exile. The third-person narrator is interspersed with first-person in the following dialogue:

> What the devil does he do in there, she had asked him
>
> "Relaxes a little, that's all. Drink a bit, reads, listens to his records."
>
> "Can't nobody spend every day in a shed for three years without being up to some devilment," she said. "I wouldn't know about that." (*Tar Baby* 13-14)

This shifting point of view allows Morrison to establish simultaneous critical and sympathetic perspectives for her characters. These shifts in turn contribute to the novel's richness as a commentary, at the same time; the shifts engage readers in a continuous process of revision of their impressions.

In the novel, the conflict is presented in the opening pages itself. Son, a tar baby rescued by woman makes him think of an alien in this land. The novel is divided into ten chapters with a prologue and epilogue. The narrative style of the prologue portrays Morrison's love of storytelling. She reveals facts slowly and through the accumulation of detail, rather than through blunt exposition. The man's identity in the prologue is not revealed, although important details can be gleaned from his context: He is black, accustomed to lying about his identity and has not heard a woman's voice for a long time. (*Tar Baby* 6)

It can be observed that Morrison has employed not only the technique of 'telling' but also of 'showing' in this novel. After a dialogue between Ondine and Sidney, Ondine goes on to explain the past of Valerian. It is a light and gregarious moment in which the narrator stays back. Despite a few chances for intrusion, the implied author 'shows' the character in a joined mood and the reader enjoys fiction on his own. The narrator does not comment either on the characters or the events of episodes of future course of action. In chapter two, which is full of flashbacks, the narrator tries to pour out the inner self of the characters. When each character is alone in his or her room, he or she can escape from the outside world and nestle deep in his or her own thoughts. Each character focuses on at least one significant personal moment from the past with the help of flash back describing how they live with the past every day even in the present. The following thoughts of Jadine about Valerian are an example:

> Where one hundred horsemen rode one hundred horses, so Valerian said.... One French soldier on a horse, not a hundred. "They are still there," he said.

> "And you can see them if you go over there at night. But I suppose we'll ever meet. If they've been riding for as long as the story is old." (*Tar Baby* 47-48)

Through an interior monologue, Jadine remembers the horsemen: "Maybe they're not old, Jadine thought, staring out the window. Maybe they're still young, still riding. One hundred men on one hundred horses…who had run her out of Paris. She crawled back into bed and tried to fix the feeling that had troubled her. (*Tar Baby* 48)

The very technique of memory which is the hallmark of Morrison's writing can be seen adequately in this novel. The memory of Sydney of Baltimore suggests the class distinctions that exist within black culture. Although he considers himself a black man from Philadelphia, proud and upwardly mobile, he remains connected to his past as a poor, southern black. Valerian and Margaret's memories indicate that there are also divisions among white people. From the first chapter, it is clear that Valerian has a more comfortable relationship with the black servants.

The struggle between nature and civilization is the theme of the novel. When Jadine almost sinks into the tar pit, a change occurs within her. She spent the day interacting with a man who does not embody civilization and also fought not to drown in a pit of tar. Jadine's struggle in the tar pit represents the island's strength over civilization. She has been literally entrapped in the slime of the swamp, overseen by natural forces that are explicitly female:

> The women looked down from the rafter of the trees and stopped murmuring. They were delighted…. This girl was fighting to get away from then… .They wondered at the girl's desperate struggle down below to be free, to be something other than they were. (*Tar Baby* 183)

These women with "ancient properties," and those the novel is dedicated to, held the community together like tar and did not consider themselves weak. The narrator emphasizes how Son, in preparing himself to enter society, removes the wildness, and also by implication the blackness, from his appearance. Jadine lacks a sense of home, as indicated by her descriptions of her hometown as Philadelphia, Baltimore, and Paris. By having two main characters move among different social settings with such disruptive consequences for their psyches, the narrator portrays the difficulty of tying oneself to a single identity firmly. The tree which Son sees when he first comes to the island, whose fruit could be poisonous or nutritious, is a metaphor for the potential Jadine holds. He eats the fruit because he cannot resist it, just as he cannot tear himself away from Jadine.

The writer makes the reader suspend the pace of time in Isle de Chevaliers, but time moves much faster in New York City. The big city is very sophisticated compared to life on the island, and therefore much more happens at a faster pace and the days fly by before Jadine and Son realize it. On Isle des Chevaliers, time moves extremely slowly, and pages pass before a single day does. The narrator shows even slower place when switching from Isle de Chevaliers to Son's small hometown of Eloe. Son's values are clear from his deep pleasure in returning to Eloe and his willingness to embrace the town's rules. For Jadine, Eloe is a nightmare of restriction and oppression. She does not understand the rules that prevent her from sleeping in Old Man's house. The role of the 'implied author' cannot be ignored in *Tar Baby*, as in every chapter the philosophical thinking of the characters is nothing but the writer herself. Note, for instance, the following advice of Ondine who defines the role of daughter Jadine, a girl has got to be a daughter first. She has to learn that. And if she never learns how to be a daughter, she can never learn to be a woman. I mean a real woman: a woman good enough for a child; good enough for a man…. A daughter is a woman that cares about where she comes from and takes care of them that took care of her. (*Tar Baby* 281)

Jadine does not want to look back. She wants to look forward, and she wants to be free to create her own identity outside of the confines of nature, race, sex, and history. She says, "There are other ways to be a woman. Nanadine.... I don't want to be like you." (*Tar Baby* 281-82)

The narrator presents fully empathetic characters with different points of view, and these views are seen here clearly. In the story of the *Tar Baby*, a white farmer makes a figure out of tar to catch a wily rabbit that wants to steal his cabbages. When the rabbit hits the scarecrow, it gets stuck in the tar. The more it struggles to escape, the more struck it gets in the sticky substance. Son thinks that he is the clever trickster and rabbit, and Jadine is the tar baby that has enticed him with fake blackness until he got snared and now cannot free himself. The reason Son cannot free himself of Jadine is because he loves her. However, for Jadine, Son is stuck in his imagination of the past, unable to free himself and clinging to the tar baby when he could just let go. What Jadine does not want to realize is that Son is tied to his roots and will never let go. The tar baby story helps to identify Son's and Jadine's true differences. It is argued that one cannot simply choose to be rooted or rootless, white or black, rich or poor. Jadine and Son are both black, but this does not make them the same. While Son is comfortable with his roots, Jadine feels more comfortable in the white European culture.

As throughout the novel, the narrator here draws a parallel between the black characters and nature itself. The novel's two protagonists, Son and Jadine, show the least change in their perspectives at this point in *Tar Baby*. At the beginning of the novel, Jadine had arrived on Isle des Chevaliers from Europe, uncertain about her goals in life and how they are related to her race and heritage. Now she is uneasily yet firmly preparing to return to Europe to pick up her career and her relationship with the white man Ryk. When she feels the burning memory of tar while passing the swamp on the way to the house, she simultaneously feels entrapped in a relationship with a backward man.

The metaphor of the reproductive cycle of the queen ant stands in for Jadine's feelings in her last appearance in the novel. The narrator intentionally leaves the final paragraph of the epilogue somewhat ambiguous. See, for instance, the last paragraph:

> "He felt around, crawled off and then stood up. Breathing heavily with his mouth open he took a few tentative steps. The pebbles made him stumble.... Then he ran. Lickety-spit. Lickety-spit. Looking neither to the left nor to the right. Lickety-spit. Lickety-spit. Lickety- lickety- lickety- spit." (*Tar Baby*, 306)

The language and context in the above paragraph suggest that the ending merges Brer Rabbit's escape from Brer Fox's trap with the blind horsemen's escape from bondage. Son ultimately chooses to join the wild men of the island. He has given up on being united with Jadine, but he has also given up on the hope of returning home to Eloe. At the most profound level, Son is first and foremost connected with nature, and ultimately, he finds his way to that part of the world to which he belongs. So, Morrison is successful in delineating the story of tar baby by taking two protagonists from different cultures. Morrison on one occasion declares that while writing *Tar Baby* she had "wished" for a happy ending. (Wilson 133) The ending seems rather ambivalent, and so some critical controversy surrounded it. On one side of the debate the ending has been called nothing less than a "muddle." (Colman 72) On the other side, it has been called an "optimistic" picture of Son's final success as a man. (Howthorne 105)

Thus, the change in the point of view, following shifts in the reader's perspective on characters and events, gives a high degree of concentration and intensity to the novel. At every moment readers need to be sensitive to the perspective developed about the various characters and situations. Morrison is, however, successful in delineating the theme through the characters of Jadine and Son. *Tar Baby* reflects her heightened consciousness. She produces a work that reflects the positive principles of traditional African society. Each of her major characters has an opportunity to present his or her particular views on self and others. And while there is an omniscient narrator, he is not given a role superior to that of each of the others. He only highlights and not prescribes or defines the thoughts and actions of significant character. Such a narrative technique definitely offers a more balanced, more objective picture.

Works Cited:

Bigsy, Christopher. 'Jazz Queen,' The Independent. 26 April 1992.

Bois, Du. The Souls of Black Folk. New York: 1969.

Coleman, James. "The Quest for Wholeness in Toni Morison's Tar Baby," Black American Literature Forum. 20 (1986): 72.

Hawthorne, Evelyn. "On Gaining the Double-Vision: Tar Baby as Diasporean Novel," Black American Literature Forum 22 (1988): 105.

LeClair, Thomas. "'The Language Must Not Sweet': A Conversation with Toni Morrison." New Republic, March 21, 1981.

Morrison, Toni, and Nellie McKay. "An Interview with Toni Morrison." Contemporary Literature 24.4 (1983): 413-429.

Morrison, Toni. Tar Baby. London: Vintage, Random House, 2004.

Rhodes, Lisa R. Toni Morrison: Great American Writer. New York: Franklin Watts, Glolier Publishing Co., Inc., 2001.

Warren, Joseph Beach. The Twentieth Century Novel: Studies in Technique. New York: The Century Company, 1932.

Wilson, Ann L. Toni Morrison's Tar Baby. Research & Education Assoc., 1998.

15. Woman Struggle in Bharati Mukherjee's *Miss New India*

Subhash Singh

Abstract: This chapter is an attempt to focus the struggle of a woman in the patriarchal society. The novel, *Miss New India* displays a life of a woman who expect to work in Call Centre, but her society try to depreciate her aspiration and force to enter the family life, from which she escapes to fulfil her dreams in foreign country. Anjali Bose, a middle-class woman from the rural Bihar town of Gauripur, is the protagonist of this novel. Anjali Bose, a resident of the Bihar town of Gauripur, is always looking for means of escaping the village's strict culture. Anjali's father has chosen Subodh Mitra as a potential husband for her. But before they got married, he had raped her. This incident stunned Anjali Bose. She made the decision to leave her home and pursue a different job because she was socially conscious. Consequently, Anjali quickly adapts to her new environment and modifies her personality, which transforms her life. She creates a place for herself and forges her own path. In contrast to her mother and sister, who compromised their fate, Anjali continues forward and manages to live and integrate into the new city. *Miss New India* is a prime example of a girl from traditional family, who struggle for her identity and individuality.

Keywords: Identity, Women, Culture and Individuality

Women novelists in Indian literature in English occupy a prominent place. Many women novelists wrote about the circumstances of women. One among them is Bharati Mukherjee. Bharati Mukherjee has left a lasting influence on the literary landscape. She was a pioneering author in both postcolonial literary studies and Indian diasporic literature. She has written eight novels namely, *The Tiger's Daughter* (1971), *Wife* (1975), *Jasmine* (1989), *Holder of the World* (1993), *Leave it to Me* (1997), *Desirable Daughters* (2002), *Tree Bride* (2004), *Miss New India* (2011) and a few short stories also authored. All of Bharati Mukherjee's speaking female characters in her works raise a woman's voice. Bharati Mukherjee is a diasporic writer who has distinguished herself among the canonical authors in America. She is an Indian-born novelist who makes Indians the heroes of her stories. Her works primarily focus on Indian immigrants struggling to make a life for themselves in a foreign country, usually America. Her novels and even short stories are written in an American setting for the most part. *Miss New India*, a recent novel by Bharati Mukherjee, stands out from all of her other works due to its Indian background. Themes like socio cultural awareness, uprooting, nostalgia, alienation, assimilation, diasporic consciousness, multiculturalism and memoirs are just a few of Bharati Mukherjee's themes. Her iconic works reflect both her own experience and the evolving nature of American culture. Sincere portrayals of her own cultural location in West Bengal, India, displacement and alienation from her native country to Canada, where she was simultaneously overexposed as a racial minority and invisible as a writer, and her final relocation and assimilation to the United States of America as a naturalized citizen are found in her novels. The sense of struggle to find a place to belong that the female protagonist of Bharati Mukherjee's works exhibits is what defines them. Mukherjee has personally gone through a terrible acculturation process.

The trilogy she started with Desirable Daughters and The Tree Bride is finished with *Miss New India*. Anjali Bose, a middle-class woman from the rural Bihar town of Gauripur, is the protagonist of this novel. Anjali Bose, a resident of the Bihar town of Gauripur, is always looking for means of escaping the village's strict culture. The author has created an image of a young woman who is restless and seeking happiness. She does not let other people determine her fate as the other Gauripur females do. She had big expectations for herself. Although she was raised in a traditional middle-class family, she aspires to a more modern way of life. She rebels because she wants freedom. The sentences that follow demonstrate her desire for independence:

> "She liked the idea of not having to go right back home to her father's bullying and her mother's tearful silence. They were obsessed with finding a respectable son-in-law who would overlook negatives such as green eyes, a stubborn personality, and a nominal dowry." (MNI, 12)

Anjali Bose is attractive, young and tall. She has a degree in commerce. Mukherjee examines the life of a young woman in India's newly established, inventive society through Anjali Bose. Indians place a greater emphasis on family, society and rituals. She realizes that leaving the family traditions is difficult for her in the Bagehot household. She is aware that although you could leave your house, family traditions cannot be abandoned. She observes the changes in Bangalore that occur throughout her life. She discovered that Gauripur is her native country while in Bagehot House, Bangalore. She is also aware of her origins. She says:

> "I have no roots anyplace yet in India. My predecessors were loathed and abused by everybody except themselves. I comprehend Sonali-di, even Baba." (MNI, 136)

The entire family prays for Anjali Bose to find a good boy. Marriage was a religious duty for her father. Anjali's father has chosen Subodh Mitra as a potential husband for her. But before they got married, he had raped her. This incident stunned Anjali Bose. She made the decision to leave her home and pursue a different job because she was socially conscious. With the assistance of her teacher, Peter Champion, she left Gauripur and arrived in Bangalore. Bangalore first enthused her, but later she becomes depressed. Anjali views employment as the key to happiness. She reasoned that whereas a job confers respect and influence, money ushers in metamorphosis. Anjali changes herself again, this time from a girl from Gauripur to a woman from Bangalore. She became aware of the changes in her life in Bangalore. *Miss New India* paints an image of India as we have never truly seen it before, both as a modern nation and as a traditional one like many others. Anjali moves to a major city, abandoning her old traditions and discovering a new identity as a modern girl with an American accent. Her name is changed from Anjali to Angie to symbolize her shift. She confesses,

> "And for the first time she was able to articulate it, at least to herself: Maybe I'm not here. Maybe I'm not suing it. "Angie" is somewhere else. Splitting herself in two was a comfort" (MNI,49-50).

Anjali Bose thinks that being Angie is really reputable and sophisticated, is the *Miss New India* and is good with the title, and Bharati Mukherjee explores this new India in her most recent novel. Anjali was portrayed by Mukherjee as socially conscious and capable of handling any situation in society.

Bharati Mukherjee has also given her description of Bangalore a touch of the colonial past. This novel depicts Bangalore as a city with a colonial past. Bangalore has a large number of locations, structures and even citizens with British ancestry and nomenclature. Anjali finds the culture of the new city confusing at first. She is shocked to see the cultural jarring. She observes the stark contrast between Bangalore's way of life and Gauripur's way of life. She begins to question her potential after meeting several young working women and girls in Bangalore. She is unable to handle the American accent. She was clueless. Strange creatures lived in the gaps between words in the English language. She catches a glimpse of Bangalore's call centre culture. She learns about the phoney identities and names used by Indian call centre employees. They pick up a flawless American accent that is not their own. They frequently change their American names. English is used by all those high-fiving, caffeinated call centre representatives with fictitious American names.

> "Darren, Will, Mike, Brad, Tom, Fred, Hank, Paul, Josh, Jeff. And Mukesh/Mickey Sharma, the sicko-caller from champagne." (MNI, 132)

Here, Bharati Mukherjee paints a picture of two distinct Indians: the first, which she realized as a young girl was full of limitations and social bondage, and the latter, which is now and offers many options for a woman to develop and carve out an identity for herself. Women in old India are confined to the four walls of their homes and are expected to adhere to the *Laxman Rekha* of morals and manners associated with the patriarchal society. However, these two aspects of ancient India and new India have been openly examined in the novel, *Miss New India*. Sonali Das, the protagonist Anjali Bose's sister, is shown as the conventional woman of old India who has been married to a man chosen by her father. Sonali Das breaks the limitations of her home and the unique constraints of society in order to build a bright and successful future for herself. The truth about India that Mukherjee shares with all American readers through *Miss New India* has the same impact on them as it did on her when she was younger and living in America. Of course, there is a dark side to the enticing draw of living in New India. It establishes independence from limitations imposed by class, caste and gender. It is not only about overcoming obstacles but also it is about reinventing oneself. The picture of societal development in India gives people something to ponder.

As a result, *Miss New India* depicts Anjali Bose's cultural shock and moral conflict as she travels from Gauripur to Bangalore to pursue her goals and confronts India's contrasted society. Anjali is aware that each country's culture is shaped by its own set of ideas and myths, eating and dressing customs, educational systems and value systems. However, within each country one can discover cultural differences by relocating from rural to urban areas from small towns to major metropolises or megacities. With all of their cultural and socioeconomic distinctions, Gauripur and Bangalore combine the two disparate realms of tradition and modernity. Consequently, Anjali quickly adapts to her new environment and modifies her personality, which transforms her life. Young women from towns and urban communities make an effort to check in with instruction up to the upper auxiliary level, despite the fact that they have not always benefited from the very basic training. Anjali is a modern metropolitan girl who possesses complete versatility. People from working-class backgrounds also benefit from being drawn to the natural world in order to keep up with their academic potential. The modern Indian woman starts looking for new routes so she can enjoy more independence and opportunities. The new woman engages in combat in order to survive in the fascinating world. Surprisingly, women have benefited from modern education after attaining freedom. A young woman from the white-collar class quickly decides on jobs with the fewest skills.

In Bangalore, the city of her dreams, she just so happened to meet Mr Girish Gujral, who encouraged her throughout her journey to acclimatize to a new way of life. He exhibited compassionate behaviour and showed Anjali Bose kindness. She honestly asked him for what she needed. After the surprise introduction of Mr G. G., she felt as though half of her aspirations had come true. Anjali could see that Mr G. G. was taking care of her with fatherly devotion and attention. He showered her with all the affection and encouragement she needed to succeed in the foreign place. She never experienced any alienation. In order to improve Anjali's interpersonal skills, Mr Peter Champion referred her to the successful call centre trainers Miss Usha Desai and Mrs Parvati Banerji. Anjali received assistance from them in all her endeavours and training to help her become a skilled customer service specialist. Anjali became familiar with Bangalore's fashions, was prepared to deal with the unpredictable shifts and made an effort to assimilate it. Despite having grown up in an aristocratic family in Gouripur. She was an unquestionably strong lady who was willing to go out and party.

Here, Bharathi Mukherjee presented the struggle of a young Indian woman as they move from a residential neighbourhood to a large city in India. She joins a group of young, incredibly motivated teenagers, who use the American language to land call centre jobs and make a living by adopting the persona of Anjali Bose. Many Indian girls who are eager to achieve great things look up to Anjali as a role model. Anjali has many good and bad experiences in the big, high-tech city before she finally reinvents herself. Bharati Mukherjee does a good job of capturing the struggle and independence of an Indian girl in her novel, *Miss New India*. Unlike prior novels, which emphasize the issues with international migration, *Miss New India* investigates the style of internal or familial resettlement and reverses migration.

Conclusion

The creation of America within India might be considered Bharati Mukherjee's goal with *Miss New India*. In Bangalore, the main character goes through the stages of estrangement, nostalgia and finally assimilation. Anjali stands in for immigrants, who have been uprooted from their homes and relocated to new locations in order to establish themselves. Anjali serves as the poster child for *Miss New India* in Bharati Mukherjee's account of the finding of the new India. Her relocation from Gauripur to Bangalore resembles a move to a foreign nation. She creates a place for herself and forges her own path. In contrast to her mother and sister, who compromised their fate, Anjali continues forward and manages to live and integrate into the new city. This is in contrast to her mother and sister. A young Indian woman who stays in her own country introduces and changes American norms and ethics in the 21st century India depicted by Bharati Mukherjee. In the novel, roots and pathways are negotiated in unusual ways, resulting in the expansion of new types of cultural identities. *Miss New India* is a prime example of a girl from a traditional family, who struggle for her identity and individuality.

Works Cited:

Alam, Fakrul, (2000). Migration and Settlement in North America in Bharati Mukherjee's Fiction, Asian American Writing, Vol. 2, Fiction. Ed. Somdatta Mandel, Prestige Books, New Delhi, pp. 61- 82.Babu, T., R., and Kumar, A., P., (2013). Feminist Perspectives in Bharati Mukherjee's Novels. International Journal of Humanities and Social Science Invention, 2 (3), 40-42.

Brewster, Anne, (2012). Nationalism in Mukherjee's Novels. Macmillan Publication, London.

Chitins, Suma. (2005). Feminism: Indian Ethos and Indian Convictions, Feminism in India, Ed. Maitrayee Chaudhuri, Zed Books New York, pp. 8-25.

Dhawan R., K., (1998). The Fiction of Bharati Mukherjee: A Critical Perspective. Atlantic Publishers, New Delhi 1998.

Manisha, Dwivedi, (2019). Reinvention of the Self: In Bharati Mukherjee's "Miss New India". Research Journal of English Language and Literature, 7 (1), 322-324.

Mukherjee, Bharati, (2012). Miss New India. Rupa Publication, New Delhi.

Philips, D., (2015). The New Miss India: Popular Fiction in Contemporary India, Women: A Cultural Review, 26 (1-2), 96-111.

Saxena, Anju, (2011). Role of Women in English Literature, Sonali Publications, New Delhi.

Shukla, S., and Banerji, N., (2014). The Theme of Alienation and Assimilation in the Novels of Bharati Mukherjee and Jhumpa Lahiri: A Socio Literary Perspective. International Journal of English and Literature, 5 (1), 19-22.

16. ELT: A Paradigm Shift in the 21st Century

Rupinder Kaur

Abstract: The present paper seeks to analyse and discuss the paradigm shift in English Language Teaching (ELT) in the 21st century with special reference to its model, methodology and pedagogy. The impact of globalization and the advancement of modern technology upon the classroom teaching of English language will be minutely analysed. The role of an ELT teacher in context of making classroom teaching more engaging, receptive and learner oriented with the employment of varied techniques and methods like multilingualism, translanguaging will be discussed in detail. ELT and its unique role in preserving the culture and identity of the students belonging to different class, culture and language will be observed in the light of novel applications. The paper will make an attempt to explore the current trends and teaching methodologies being used in ELT globally. It will also touch upon the relationship between ELT and the demands of the contemporary age.

Keywords: ELT, Globalization, Technology, Multilingualism, Translanguaging, ICT, Methodology, Pedagogy, Teacher, Student.

Introduction

English language teaching has been the subject of discourse since it was introduced as a medium of education and instruction in all the educational institutions across the globe. The English being the colonizers left an indelible mark upon the countries it was ruling in context of their literature and more so in language. Due to the expanse of the British Empire every country embraced and ended up with English as the most natural companion to their native language. The sun may have set on the British Empire but it is still shining on the English Language. As it has been rightly remarked "...English has ceased to be the language of its native speakers only—it has already attained the stature of a world language." (T.C. Baruah, 5). Jack C. Richards of the similar view that, "English today has a unique status, as a consequence of the role it plays around the world and its function as an 'international' or 'world language'. It has been described as the world's lingua franca." (Jack C. Richards, 4)

Keeping in view the stature of this language at present, the teaching of English language has become more complex with the advent of globalization. Globalization has not only introduced a plethora of methodologies to impart the nuances of this language but has also paved the way for making more experiments with the learners to make language learning simpler and more comprehensible. As it has been rightly observed by Jack C. Richards:

> "...there has been a dramatic change in the scope of English language teaching worldwide and an increasing demand for competent English language teachers, as well as for language programmes that can deliver the English language skills and competencies needed by today's global citizens." (Jack C. Richards, 4)

The more world has evolved in terms of globalization the more teaching of English language has evolved. "...the clear need arises to reinvigorate or re-introduce English language teaching in schools and training colleges..." (Randolph Quirk,10).

All the three world countries namely developed, developing and under developed have marked a great change in the learning and acquisition of this language. It has become the epitome of globalization, technology and business.

IELTS and ELT

Initially the dream of foreign education was only open to the meritorious or affluent students. But with the liberal policies of foreign lands in inviting the students from other countries lead to the mushrooming of this language all across the world. All the aspiring candidates are given academic and educational opportunity via sitting for IELTS in their home country and passing it with requisite band scores as prescribed by the foreign countries in their immigration policies. It has taken a sweep to the extent that third world countries where the students are aspiring to be a part of mainstream foreign education has somewhat forsaken the courses offered by her home country in quest for better job and financial security.

Earlier the teaching of English for the competitive exams for both global and home was highly based on the objective type questions or more so it was for composition purpose. The innumerous registration of the students to sit for IELTS altogether brought an instrumental change in the teaching of English language. The methodology and pedagogy of learning English language has become more unique and aim oriented. The conventional English teachers are replaced by the facilitators who could help the students to bring the desired band score. The students are taught in a capsule where they achieve their proficiency in all the four pillars of English namely Listening Speaking Reading and Writing.

Multilingualism in ELT

In the past more emphasis was laid upon the direct method of teaching English. It was being taught in the schools and universities across the globe in the same manner as it is taught to the native speakers of this language. This attempt created more chaos than solving the function of teaching English in more comprehensive and meaningful way. This method became eventually troublesome process especially for both the students and the teachers who had this language as their second language. The need was to bring about a meaningful change in the method of teaching to enhance the understanding level rather escalating the confusion developing from direct method. The said change was proposed by J.C. Catford who in his paper the teaching of English as a foreign language :

> "The teaching of English as a secondary language..., is the process of creating English using bilinguals .... and the problems involved, and the principles underlying this process, are different from those relating to the teaching of English to native speakers of English." (J.C Catford, 138)

The essential requirement to make English language more accessible, friendly and unilateral has added more dimensions to the teaching of this language. The world has gone a step further by making English open to use of multilingual method of instruction to make students more interested in the chapter being delivered. The concept of multilingualism was foreign to the concept of English language teaching. As the classrooms across the world are becoming more heterogeneous in terms of culture, nationalities and languages, the incorporation of multilingual methodology would carve a niche for synergy and compatibility. We may say the multilingual method of teaching where the students are allowed to use their mother tongue along with other languages known to him builds required motivation among the student community to learn and excel in the target language. The role of the teacher has become more challenging in this context "...every teacher of English should be informed with knowledge and understanding of both the mother-dialect of the pupils and of the national or regional language of culture being made available to them." (J.L.M. Trim, 83)

This process may foster the spirit among the students to take pride in their culture and ethnicity. Therefore we may say that English language is not only being used as a medium to teach but at the same time it is bridging the gap between the various cultures and different ethnic groups which were earlier not taken into consideration while teaching of this language.

ICT and ELT

The virtual platforms are also mushrooming to cater to the needs of the learners which cannot be realized in the conventional classroom teaching. "Classroom teaching alone is not sufficient to achieve the objectives of teaching English." (T.C. Baruah, 334) Technology and Computer has brought about a sea change in the arena of English language learning and teaching. It would not be an exaggeration to say that Information and communication technology (ICT) has begun a new era in the field of imparting education and has developed more innovative methods and trends in teaching of English. To grow as professional and to make a mark in the teaching of this language a teacher has to be equally equipped with the technical know-how. The online platform in the form of Facebook, Instagram and the various applications introduced by the top-notch organizations like Podcast, Grammar based application and BBC Learning English has made English language more accessible and more functional in context of its learning and applications. The technology has touched upon all the spheres of applications. The concept of online teaching and learning has put English language in a more progressive state in the recent innovations and developments in technology and research. All the rare and old literature of the world has been digitalized and is accessible on the click of a button. Much software has been developed to support not only teaching of English but also English in general. The advancement of technology has not made the learning of English as outdated but has added a new dimension to its present way of language learning.

Virtual Reality and Augmented Reality

The concept of Virtual reality is now being active the arena of English language teaching as the students of the class will be able to visit the historical English eminent landmarks while sitting in their respective classroom. It is the perfect example of a world classroom. It would be more of an experiential learning.

Augmented reality is yet another dimension to the digital display of the environment we are living in. In other words, it is the extension of the real world with the use of modern technology "Pokemon GO" is the famous example of augmented reality it has made the learning experience more hi-tech and interesting. The expansion of digital literacy among the students and the coming future generation will make language learning and acquisition more fun and receptive. The application of augmented reality in the classroom will not only strengthen their retention power in terms of vocabulary building but will also keep their level of motivation high. It will be a rich source for the tech savvy to excel in language learning and would be a great supplementary advantage for the teachers to cater to the sense thirst and imagination of the students.

Netflix and ELT

Netflix of late has got attention of the young minds and people who are interested to watch the plays, stories and cinematic adaptations of the text of their choice. It can be a great source to enhance one's passive listening skills. As listening is the foundation for speaking. It can prove to be a major trend in learning a language. However, one cannot overlook the fact that it may not prove to be a comprehensive platform to increase student's language proficiency. A teacher's guidance and monitoring in making Netflix as a source of language building in the classroom can do wonders in the arena of ELT teaching.

Instagram and ELT

Many ELT teachers have broken the barriers of traditional classroom teaching by making social media platforms like Instagram as a rich source to impart essential short lessons. It has made the teaching more engaging and effective. It is true of the short lessons but for the comprehensive classes it may not be of great worth. By simply following key hash tags such as #build vocabulary one can easily access the short and terse lessons. It is a new wave in the digital education as it may save their time on social media doing more meaningful activity rather than spending hours in scrolling down unimportant data.

Task Based Learning

Gone are the days when English language learning was confined to one text and the probable questions as per the syllabus. Constant efforts are being made to make the teaching of English more practical and innovative. Task-based learning is one such activity where the students enhance their learning in collaboration with meaningful and communicative task. The practical aspect of any subject provides more impetus and importance to its existence. The efforts are being made by the ELT teachers in this direction by devising purpose-driven activities. The success ratio if these activities are highly dependent upon the effective planning and execution of these activities. It can only be successful if it could have direct impact on the real world, we are living in.

Linguistic Landscape

Linguistic landscape is a new ELT aspect of this age. Linguistic landscape is the way in which the learners are introduced to the language as per the given environment or surroundings. It involves public spaces, places of worship, government offices, classrooms and even our homes. The target language can be present on sign boards, notice board, clothing, advertisements. The awareness of the varied language encompassing our everyday life can motivate the students to learn and use them. Moreover, it is more practical aspect of enriching one's language proficiency just by the tool of observation. A teacher can assign students with the task of observing their surrounding in reference to the languages and the context in which it is being used. They may be asked to come up with their individual observation and the number of languages that are used. It influences the learning of the students and make them more agile and sensitive towards language learning.

Translanguaging and ELT

Translanguaing is a new method of incorporating various languages of the students apart from using the target language. It has brought about a fundamental change in the process of teaching and at the same time has decolonized the ELT classrooms. It has lightened the cognitive load of the students and has democratized language weight age. The concept of translanguaging has broadened the perspective of every ELT teacher. Previously, it was believed that the best method to teach English was to never to use the native language. However, with many observations and research at global level it has been realised that the use of students native language actually helps in the acquisition of English language. Students feel more relaxed and motivated when they can freely use their language while learning English language.

They use the best resources from their native language to understand English in their ELT classes. At the same time the students are able to retain their individuality and social identity through the use of shared language. It makes a classroom a playground for global communication as it foreshadows the uniqueness of each culture and society. it facilitates the process of communication and sharing of ideas.

ELT and Research

The most conspicuous instance of use of ICT can be traced in research and innovation sector where the participants across the globe come on a single platform via Webinars. It is most viable and convenient form of platform among the geographically scattered people. The advent of Zoom, Teams, Google Meet in information and technology sector has broadened the umbrella of participants which was impossible at the time of physical seminars. The more diverse is the participation the more ideas and wonderful perspectives one can share on the common platform. The rigidity of the past and the exclusivity of the conferences and seminars have now been addressed effectively with the inclusivity of people around the world.

Communicative Language Teaching

The responsibility of a teacher has widened in all terms in not only making students equipped in written and reading aspects of the language but also the communicative aspects of the English language. Communicative language teaching came into being when the world saw a great change in the restructuring of recruitment process of all the MNC across the globe. The people working in offices are not confined to one specific region as it was earlier. The people are geographically scattered and the common thread of English makes it possible for them to communicate effectively with each other. Looking at the trends various universities, private and Govt. institutions took this onus to make their students well versed in the gamut of conversational English. The concept of language lab in the universities and government and private institutions has been a yet another addition in making the ELT more practical and to be in the right sync with the age in which we are living. The emergence of language lab has given a great impetus to learning of this language predominantly in speaking part as phonetics is also taught and practiced to bring the desired change in the diction, stress and intonation of the students. The language laboratory individualizes the process of learning and makes teaching effective. The responses of the students can be stored in his assigned computer and at the same time he can look for the answers. The participation of the student is more as language lab is not confined to theoretical facet of the language but it duly caters to the needs of the global citizen which is the ability to communicate effectively and intelligently in any given scenario.

ELT and Current Practices in Teaching Text

The teaching of English has been revolutionized throughout the world as Shakespeare is now not confined to books but many teaching pedagogies are being put into practice to make it more retainable in the minds of the readers. The various activities that could be employed to teach drama or poetry are pre-listening, post-listening, pre-reading, post-reading, quiz, enactment of the play in the classroom itself through role play have been extensively applied in the classroom right from the nascent stage of education. The cinematic adaptations of the novels and dramas by famous writers have revived interest of the student and general public in literature. Literature and its related conventional genres are no more the source of reference or part of curriculum but has crossed the boundaries from their classrooms to their living rooms.

ELT and World

The demand of CELTA and TEFL teachers across the globe in the 21st century both online and offline has validated the relevance of English language as Lingua franca. The Middle Eastern and European countries have too acknowledged the pertinent role being played by the English language across the globe therefore the need to have well trained teachers for their schools and colleges has risen. The various elite organizations like British Council and Cambridge University etc. run such globally recognized programs for the teachers who aspire to work in foreign lands.

ELT and Rapport Building

A transformation in the methods of ELT has also made the relationship between the students and the teacher more congenial and compatible. The age-old method of teaching English which was predominantly teacher cantered after an observation was found "Teacher-cantered instruction is now admitted to lead to poor language performance. It is said to prevent student's educational growth." (Duckworth, 2009) The efforts are being made in every way to make language learning more interactive. The major objective of every language teacher is to make the atmosphere more conducive for learning and to a great extent the new methodology has bridged the yawning gap between a teacher and the student. The student now doesn't hesitate to approach his teacher. ELT has also changed the role of a teacher in the classroom as she acts more as a facilitator than a traditional teacher. "No new technique of teaching is worth trying until the confidence between the English teacher and his pupils is fully established..." (B.C. Brookes, 115)

In the light of the above statement it may be inferred that the pedagogy and methodology may only be successful if the teacher and student will share an equation where the teacher is more amiable, approachable and motivational in making her learners take keen interest in the language learning and acquisition.

Conclusion

To conclude we may say that the role of an ELT teacher in the 21st century has undergone an exponential change. The methods and pedagogies employed by ELT have made the learning process more engaging, interesting and globally relevant. To survive in this ever-dynamic environment an ELT teacher has to be abreast with the latest technology, methodology and research to make the teaching learning process more productive and relevant in the present scenario. Keeping an eye on these ELT methods and current trends, a teacher can bring about revolutionary change in making her classroom a global village where all the people from different cultures can embrace this language willingly without forsaking their own identity and culture.

Works Cited:

Baruah, T.C. The English Teacher's Handbook Sterling Publishers Private Limited; New Delhi, 1984https://www.cambridge.org/files/4914/4353/3927/9781107456105_excerpt.pdf

Richards, Jack C. The Key Issues in Language Teaching Cambridge University Press; United Kingdom, 2015.

Quirk, Randolph and A.H. Smith Ed. The Teaching of English Oxford University Press; London, 1964.Quirk, Randolph and A.H. Smith Ed. The Teaching of English Oxford University Press; London, 1964

Quirk, Randolph and A.H. Smith Ed. The Teaching of English Oxford University Press; London, 1964.

Baruah, T.C. The English Teacher's Handbook Sterling Publishers Private Limited; New Delhi, 1984. https://www.fluentu.com/blog/educator-english/english-language-teaching/

DuckWorth, E. (2009). Helping Students Get to Where Ideas Can Find Them. The New Educators, 5, 185-188.

Quirk, Randolph and A.H. Smith Ed. The Teaching of English Oxford University Press; London, 1964. https://www.researchgate.net/publication/329698569_English_Language_Teachinghttp://puneresearch.com/english/search? word=english+ language+ teaching&submit=SUBMT

17. Use of ICT Tools in Learning -Teaching Outcomes For 21st Century Digital Age Learners

Meenakshi

Abstract: As a result of the digital revolution, today's pupils and students may find traditional activities, such as reading, exceedingly uninteresting, whereas they are naturally drawn to audio-visual information (e.g., videos, photos, and audio resources). In this digital era, Information and Communication Technology (ICT) can enable, support, and reinforce the introduction of new pedagogical practices that comply with the educational demands of the twenty-first-century knowledge society. On the other hand, educators most often receive a traditional education, and may feel unprepared to communicate with their students using digital jargon and Hence studying the issues and challenges related to ICT use in teaching and learning can assist teachers in overcoming the obstacles and become successful technology users However, despite this potential and despite the delivering of skills-based professional development & the increase in the level of ICT infrastructure, teachers are more often reluctant rather than willing to use ICT.

Introduction: The main purpose of this study is to analyze teachers' perceptions of the challenges faced in using ICT tools. It is hoped that the outcome of this research provides proper information and recommendation to those responsible for integrating new technologies into the teaching and learning process. Then from this research, it can contribute to the development of the field of education, especially for teachers, who are required to be better and explore more deeply, especially in ICT skills and teaching styles, so that student learning outcomes can experience significant development. information and recommendation to those responsible for integrating new technologies into the teaching and learning process.

Effectively integrating information and communication technologies into teaching and learning plays an essential competency for teachers in the 21st century. Digitally literate educators can leverage technologies to increase teaching efficiency, facilitate meaningful learning and enable students to construct real-world knowledge However, the International Computer and Information Literacy Study 2018 (ICLS 2018) revealed that, on average across nations, less than half of teachers reported frequent use of ICT when teaching, and nearly two-thirds of teachers have insufficient ICT skills (Fraillon et al., 2020). Accordingly, teacher training institutions play an essential role in equipping future teachers with concrete ICT knowledge and skills (Goktas et al., 2009). Teacher education programs have made some efforts such as offering standalone educational technology courses, integrating educational technology throughout the curriculum, and providing field technology-based experiences (Nelson & Hawk, 2020; Ottenbreit-Leftwich et al., 2018; Sang et al., 2010). Despite these efforts, most PSTs enter the profession without sufficient skills and confidence in creating technology-enhanced learning environments for students.

Benefits to Learn ICT Skills: To Get a sense of the most important new technologies, as well as the expanding trend of incorporating ICT is used into education. Moreover ICT Discover about the most relevant social media platforms and how they may be used in education and learning; It also Acquire skills in how to use photos and videos in your classroom and how to make them; We Gain an understanding of how to create a website or a blog quickly and easily; Become competent in the fundamentals of developing an e-learning platform; We also Grasp about the most engaging, motivating, and innovative apps and web solutions for making education more engaging, motivating, and inventive; We also get to learn innovative techniques and best practices to integrate new technology into education by gaining a fresh perspective on ICT tools.

Models of Access to ICT Engagement :

Appropriateness of technology	Social-cultural factors
Local economic environment	Physical access to technology
Affordability of technology and technology use	Political will and public support
Locally relevant content, applications, and services	Human capacity and training

Key Issues to Remember Concerning to the Importance of ICT in Education

ICT Brings Inclusion: - The advantage of ICT in education is that all the students can learn from the course materials using ICT tools to their educational requirements. Despite this, it opens up new problems related to the 'digital divide' and provides those who are less fortunate with access to ICT resources and tools.

E-Learning or Online Learning: - Online or E-learning is getting popular as Different extraordinary events are happening in our lives, opening up opportunities to ensure that students can access course materials from anywhere, anytime.

ICT Enhances Subject Learning: - In education, ICT adds a huge value to key learning areas like numeracy and literacy.

ICT Use Motivation Learning: - The demand of society for new technology has not left out children and their requirements. With new technology, children are fascinated, motivating and encouraging

ICT in Education Improves Engagement and Knowledge Retention: - Students become more involved in their work if the TCT is integrated into lessons. And the reason behind that is the technology as a result of this increased business, it is said that they are capable to retaining knowledge more efficiently and effectively.

ICT Use Encourages Collaboration: Naturally, ICT brings children together so that it turns opens communication avenues that lead to the development of language.

ICT Use Develops ICT Literacy and ICT Capability: - ICT literacy and ICT capability are the skills of the 21st century which are best developed in ICT and remain transparent in the subject learning context.

Different ICT Tools for various Areas :

Developing Literacy

There are various tools for developing literacy:

Drawing and graphics programs	Web searching
Web creation and design	Wikis
Digital video	Word processing
Emails	Blogs

ICT tools to promote literacy and language development in early childhood education:

Word processors	Internet
Computers	Developmentally appropriate programs

There are various ICT tools for primary schools:

Spreadsheets	Animation
Presentation software	Publishing programs
Blogging	Web 2.0
Information literacy skills	Making a video

Various ICT tools for Quizzing/Testing/Gaming:

BookWidgets	Flipgrid	Plickerss
Gimkit	Deck.toys	MasteryConnect
Classtools	Formative	Lightsail
Genial.ly	Educaplay	H5P
Google forms	Flubaroo	Kahoot
Classmarker	Gynzy	JeopardyLabs

There are various types of an ICT tool for presentation:

SlideShare	Nearpod
Buncee	Peardeck
Prezi	Sutori
Prowise	Lesson up
Google slides	Mentimeter

There are various ICT Tools for studying:

Cram	Vocabulary
WRTS	Learningpod
Cobocards	Studyblue

There are various other important tools for ICT:

FeedbackFruits, HP Reveal, Class123, Diigo, Evernote, Classdojo, Delicious, iRubric, PDF Pro

Classroomscreen,me, Voicethread

The ICT devices are the latest tools, concepts and techniques used in student-to-teacher, student-to-student interaction for example: - clicker devices, mobile applications, flipped classroom) for information and communication technology.

To unlock the potential of technologies to use in the classroom, we need to do the following:

*Establish a starting point for the ICT learning of each student and integrate formative evaluation into key learning areas like literacy and numeracy in a primary school.

*Planning for progress in ICT learning progress in the learning curriculum of the Australian curriculum.

*Evidence-based on ICT learning along with the subject learning.

ICT ENABLED TOOLS FOR EFFECTIVE TEACHING LEARNING PROCESS

Following tools are used in the Teaching learning process in Online-Offline mode of instruction. During lockdown these ICT tools proved to be a boon for making the teaching learning process easy and accessible to all students.

[Learning management system (MOODLE and Google classroom):

Google Classroom - Blended Learning Platform:

Google Forms

Significance of Information and Communication Technology Integration

However, the practical employability of technology in teaching-learning practices is yet to be achieved in Pakistan. Prior studies have highlighted several benefits of integrating ICT into our education system (see 1), which are characterized below.

Teachers' Self-Efficacy

Based on the self-efficacy perspective, effective integration of ICT in education highly depends upon teachers' self-efficacy (Guoyan et al., 2021), as self-efficacy is a vital force that enables a teacher to acquire students' learning outcomes successfully. Considering the importance of teachers' self-efficacy in an effective ICT integration, several studies have suggested developing their pedagogical and technological skills by establishing training programs. The study by Khan and Abid (2021) revealed that the paradigm shift from face-to-face to online teaching-learning during the COVID-19 phase gave an advantage for teachers and students to acquire technological skills by using different digital tools and platforms. They also advocated employing an online certification decision matrix (OCDM) to assure online teaching effectiveness and readiness of teachers.

Furthermore, the findings by Aslam et al. (2021) revealed that ICT integration enhances the quality of the teaching-learning process and found a significant correlation between teachers' technological pedagogical and content knowledge (TPACK) and their technological competencies. In addition, Abbasi et al. (2021) identified positive attitudes of teachers toward applying technology in their instructional practices and identified a significant association between technology use with their technological competencies.

Students' Learning

Teacher plays an important role in cultivating successful students'

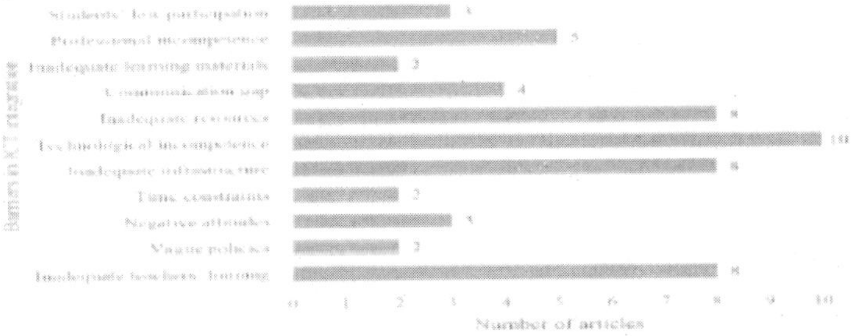

https://www.frontiersin.org/files/Articles/920317/fpsyg-13-920317-HTML/image_m/fpsyg-13-920317-g005.jpg

online learning. ICT utilization in teaching-learning practices enables a student to make meaningful use of technologies in education by accessing, selecting, establishing, and interpreting the information. Its effective integration helps in meeting the learners' educational needs by providing creative solutions to different types of learning inquiries (Rafi et al., 2019). Several studies also showed a significant relationship between technology usage in educational practices and students' academic achievement (Asif et al., 2020; Abbasi et al., 2021). Furthermore, to enhance students' creative thinking and academic performance, Ali et al. (2018) advocated that cloud computing facilitates students' learning efficiently with better adaptability in a cost-effective way. As adoption of cloud services help educational institutions to fulfil students' learning needs without having all resources, such as multimedia equipment, software, and hardware. In addition, the application of ICT in classrooms provides a motivating environment for students and keeps them engaged in educational activities (Jogezai et al., 2018). Furthermore, the disruptive phase of COVID-19 brought an opportunity to enhance the effectiveness of teaching-learning practices through ICT integration at the school level. During COVID-19, when face-to-face learning opportunities were interrupted due to schools' closure, the integration of ICT via social media platforms helped learners to continue their learning activities (Jogezai et al., 2021).

'Barriers in Information and Communication Technology Integration

The application of technology in educational practices is not a new phenomenon in developed countries. However, its applicability is still not a common practice across developing nations like Pakistan. In this regard, teachers' perceptions regarding barriers to technology integration in their teaching practices were seen in multiple studies.

Conclusion

The systematic review affirms that teachers exhibit adequate acceptance of ICT in teaching-learning practices and assist learners in acquiring learning objectives in several ways, which is why inevitable at all educational levels. However, technology use at the secondary school level is still found at the initial stages than at the higher level. Still, the changes brought by the COVID-19 pandemic brought an opportunity to enhance the effectiveness of teaching-learning practices through ICT integration at all levels. Findings also specified several barriers that hinder effective technology integration in teaching-learning practices, including lack of resources, leadership support, accessibility of ICT infrastructure, inadequate time, unclear policies, professional development, technical support, and lack of appropriate pedagogical models. In this context, concerned authorities should work on the needs and gaps which hinder educational practices from effective technology integration to acquire maximum benefits from technology-integrated teaching and learning.

Works Cited:

Zhuo, Zhang a. Yukiko Maeda a, Timothy Newby a, Zui Cheng b, Qian *Xua -The effect of preservice teachers' ICT integration self-efficacy beliefs on their ICT competencies: The mediating role of online self-regulated learning strategies https://www.sciencedirect.com/science/article/pii/S0360131522002445*

https://www.sciencedirect.com/science/article/pii/S0360131522002445

J Ola Lindberg, Anders D Olofsson, Göran. *FranssonContrasting views: Student and teacher perceptions on ICT in educationhttps://* scholar.google.co.in/scholar?q= teachers+ perception+ of+ict+in+education&hl=en&as_sdt=0&as_vis=1&oi=scholar

Akram, Huma, Abbas Hussein Abdelrady, Ahmad Samed Al-Adwan3 and Muhammad *Ramzan4Teachers' Perceptions of Technology Integration in Teaching-Learning Practices: A Systematic Review*https://www.frontiersin.org/articles/10.3389/fpsyg.2022.920317/full#F4

https://eric.ed.gov/?id=EJ1096028

https://scholar.google.co.in/scholar?q= teachers+ perception+of+ ict+in+education&hl=en&as_sdt=0&as_vis=1&oi=scholart

Orana, Velarde. *Online Teaching Tools to Enrich Your Virtual Classroomhttps*://visme.co/blog/online-teaching-tools/

Jindal, Nitin. *A List of ICT Tools for Teaching and Learning*https://leadschool.in/blog/a-list-of-ict-tools-for-teaching-and-learning-lead

18. Role of Poetry In Learning English

Shivani Dhawan

Abstract: Language and literature are inseparable. They are complementary to each other. No literature lives without language and no language survives without literature. Teaching language through literature benefits the students in learning the different genres of literature i.e. Poetry, Fiction, Drama, Essays, and Criticism. Poetry places a great demand on the reader's sensibility, sensitivity and concentration. It has an intricate pattern of words which opens myriad interpretations, new meanings and dimensions. It would not be sufficient if a teacher possesses mere proficiency in language and facility of expression. One has to hone one's skills and develop a keen sense of perception and get a 'hang' of poetry with extensive reading.

Keywords: Foreign language, Lingua-Franca, sensibility, Aesthetic Sense, Diction.

> 'Poetry is the blossom and the fragrance
> of all human knowledge, human thoughts,
> human passions, emotions language.

Poetry is not to be taught. It can be read, appreciated, memorized, written occasionally and it can always be enjoyed. Poetry and prose reveal glimpses of English literature. According to Chatfield, "Poetry is the music of thought, conveyed to us in the beauty of language." Poetry is different from prose. S.T. Coleridge once defined prose as "Words in their best order" and poetry as "The best words in their best order". Poetry feeds and waters the desires and passions instead of drying them up. F.L Billows says in the book, "Techniques of Teaching Language"-

> "We can compare prose to walking, moving from one place to another on the surface of the earth, getting the world's daily work done; poetry may be compared then to dancing, rising above the surface of the earth, getting a fuller view of its reality".

Poetry unfolds before us a whole wonderland of fairies and flowers. It develops a sense of values in human life. With good poetry, our mind is made aware of a highly disciplined order of things. Poetry is the distillation of many imagined and strangely felt experiences. Poetry is inescapable in a child's mind. In the nursery, poetry is for recreation; it is a shared experience without purpose beyond the delight it brings to the maker. Hopkins aptly remarked:

> "To do Eurydice any kind of justice, you must not slovenly read it with eyes, but with your tears".

Poetry comes to life as naturally as leaves to branches. Poetry is the first speech of human beings. Man is as much a rational animal with a mind to be enlightened as an emotional creature with needs to be satisfied. Prose appeals to the intellect, poetry to the emotions. The nursery rhymes are the only gateway through which the child enters the realm of poetry. The traditional rhyme and jingles of childhood are learnt without much apparent effort Children love musical beats which work upon the more instinctive and less conscious aspects of their nature. In the secondary school stage, pupils are required to read poetry intelligently and to participate in the appreciation of it.

Poetry is that aspect of language that fundamentally provides entertainment to the readers. It should be taught with the aims given below-

1 To give practice listening to the recitation of a poem.

2 To help the students recite a poem in a proper way.

3 To make the students understand the beauty of thought contained in the poem.

4 To enable the students to appreciate the poem by awakening in them aesthetic qualities of expression.

5 To help them improve their power of imagination.

6 To develop a love of the students for the English language.

7 To make the students familiar with the background of the poem.

8 To make the students pick up the structure or pattern

of a sentence.

9 And above all, to make the students understand the poem.

The following Principles should be kept in mind while teaching a poem—

1. Model recitation by the teacher is very essential because it helps in attracting the students toward the poem. They are able to grasp the meanings contained in the poem.

2. Detailed explanations of lines or ideas should be avoided.

3. The verbal peculiarities of the language should not be discussed. In the poems, we have words like hath, thou, thee etc. The spellings of some words are written differently. They should not be taken up too seriously as far as the study of the poem is concerned.

4. Paraphrasing the poem should be avoided. It should not be put in the form of prose.

5. The teacher should try to bring enthusiasm and zeal into the teaching of the poem.

6. As far as possible, the poem should be taught as a whole. It should be approached as a total work of art.

The present position of teaching poetry in Indian schools is not satisfactory. Teaching poetry is not everybody's cup of tea. There are very few teachers who have a real love for poetry. The group of thinkers emphasizes that poetry in English is very important and it should be given due place in the school curriculum. Poetry is an important mode of expression in language. Without the study of poetry, a person cannot be considered to be well-read in language. Poetry is that aspect of the English language that fundamentally provides entertainment to the readers.

There is something wrong that many students do not develop a love for poetry during their school or college days. Poetry is an art and the reason for including it in the school curriculum is to develop the aesthetic sense. Our aim in teaching poetry should be to give pleasure. Poetry should be "felt in the blood and felt along the heart" in the words of Wordsworth. After the intensive study of more serious subjects like mathematics and science, poetry gives variety to the work. In our sorrowful world of ours, where everything is in chaos, one must learn to recognize and appreciate the beauty and set one's face against the ugliness of the mechanical world. Very few teachers are interested in teaching poetry. They are unable to do justice to the teaching of a poem. The details of the situation are as under—

1 Some teachers ask the children to bring the poetry book to the classroom. The teachers just translate the poem into the mother tongue. They feel that in doing so they have done their duty.

2 The teachers ask the students to learn the summary of the poem from the guide. They never ask the children to purchase or study the poetry poem. Thus, many a time, the students pass the examination without having seen even the poetry book prescribed for them.

3 A few teachers of English dictate notes on poetry to the children. Then they ask them to cram the material and reproduce the same in the class orally or in written form.

4 A very limited number of teachers are able to teach a poem satisfactorily. They can recite the poem well and they are able to give training in poem recitation to the learners. Their teaching attracts the students. They are able to understand the poem really. Only their learners can say with confidence they have been taught

poetry well.

At present poetry is not properly handled by the teacher for the following reasons as pointed out by L.A.G.Strong in his essay "Poetry in the School"—

1 The teacher disliked it.

2 The teacher has been embarrassed by it.

3 The teacher has been suspicious of all forms of emotion.

4 The teacher has been indifferent to poetry and has remained satisfied in mainly paraphrasing the poems and preparing the students for examinations.

5 The teacher has loved it uncomprehendingly and for irrelevant reasons.

The teacher should therefore firmly guard against his own weakness to tackle a poetry class. While selecting a poem, attention should be given to those which are easy to understand. Poems with unusual, archaic, difficult language and thought should be avoided.

Tools that a teacher requires to teach poetry-

It would not be sufficient if a teacher possesses mere

proficiency in English and a facility of expression. One has to hone one's skills and develop a keen sense of perception and get a "hang" of poetry with extensive reading. As teachers, we need to use the tools of criticism that Eliot spoke of. In order to appreciate a poem, we need to compare, analyze, and show the students how the diction differs from one poem to another. We need to illustrate this by giving succinct examples. It could be Chaucer's language which has its moorings in old English; the intellectualization of thought in Donne or the lofty elevated high sounding words that befits Milton's epic verse; the simple lyricism of a poem like Daffodils; the terrifying shift from contemporary politics to legendary symbolism of Yeat's " The Second Coming" or the concept of birth, death, and spiritual concerns in Eliot's " The Journey of the Magi". It is pertinent that we should overcome the temptation to foist our personal prejudices while teaching English poetry. A teacher must teach Dryden with the kind of zest that perhaps he/she accords to a poem of Wordsworth. A teacher must harness the same enthusiasm in deciphering the imagery of Tennyson's "Tears, idle tears as in paying glowing tributes to Shakespeare's craft in a sonnet 'Shall I compare thee". It is imperative that we set aside our personal prejudices, remain objective and critically appreciate each poem without any bias. Only then as a teacher can do justice not only to poetry but also to our role as teachers of poetry.

There are the following Recommendations for teaching Poetry -

A-Teacher —A teacher of English poetry must be a scholar of English literature. He should be a man of poetic temperament and possess a keen insight into human life. Regarding the qualifications of the teachers of English, the conference of Professors of English in New Delhi made the following recommendations- 'The minimum qualification for the teaching of English in high schools shall be a bachelor of Arts degree followed by a teacher's training diploma in English'.

B-Selection of Poems—Poems prescribed for the schools' children should be easy and simple and language should be musical. Secondary school children should be taught poems of patriotism, nature and simple human emotions. In the middle stage, narrative poems should be introduced. Poems should be selected by expert teachers and learned educationists. Such poems should be selected from the works of well-known poets, representing various kinds of poetry such as ballads, lyrics, sonnets, odes and elegies.

C-Examination –The mode of questions set in the High School Certificate Examination should change to an appreciative form. The final assessment should not be based entirely on external examinations. Internal tests and school records should be taken into consideration. The purpose of such examinations should be to test the critical ability of the students.

D-Library-The library of a school must be made the most attractive place in the school so that the students will be drawn easily towards it. Students should have free access to books of criticism, anthologies, journals, biographies of poets, collected poems and periodicals. Teachers should help the students in selecting English poems.

E-Cocurricular Activities- A sense of appreciation for poetry can be created among the students through co-curricular activities. Arranging regular poetry recitation competitions, and encouraging students to write English poems and translate them into English simple poems from their mother tongue can develop a love for poetry in students. Dramatic versions of the poems can be enacted by students. Students may learn better intonation and widen their knowledge of English poetry by attending lectures delivered by scholars of English literature. The film shows on dramatic versions of long narrative poems that can be arranged periodically. Students should be amply rewarded for English recitals and eloquence. All these activities will broaden the cultural and literary outlook of students.

Conclusion: English plays an important role in every sphere of life as a 'Lingua Franca', Knowledge Bank', Official Language and 'Employment Passport'. It is an international language and was given the crown of supremacy. Poetry places a great demand on the reader's sensibility, sensitivity and concentration. Poetry is a kind of liberal education itself, addressed not merely to pupils in school and colleges but to the entire society. The business of poetry is not merely to convey information, it expects the reader to understand the impulses, the vibrations and the compulsions experienced by the poet. So, the best poetry is that which opens itself to infinite suggestions.

Works Cited:

Aslam, M. "Teaching of English". New Delhi: Cambridge University

Press,2008, Print.
Bhimrao, P. "Methods and Approaches of English Language Teaching in India" A paper presented in "International Conference on Recent Innovations in Science, Humanities and Management", 2017. Web.
CBSE, New Delhi, "*Language Skill Outlook; Functional English*" Class XI, 2023 Pdf.
CIFL, Hyderabad. "*Modern English Grammar and Usage*". Block 1. 1, 1995.Web.
Coleridge, S.T. "*Biography Literaria*" XV 4.
Dhand H , "*Techniques of Teaching*" New Delhi: Ashish Publishing House,1990. Print.
Hudson, W. H. "*Introduction to English Literature*".
Leavis, F.R. ''*New Beginning in English Poetry*".
Pathak P.D, "*Teaching of English in India*" 6 th edition, Agra: Vinod Pustak Mandir 1975.

19. Experiencing Self-Centric Ethics in Selected Poems of Ted Hughes

Jaswinder Kaur

Abstract: Ted Hughes is preoccupied with the fate of human culture. To him, the present cultural crisis in the Western world directly results from an over-reliance on rationalism, science and technology as the only way to a valid knowledge of reality. Throughout his poetic venture, he mocks the present egotistic ethos which views man at the centre of the universe and the earth existing solely for his use and abuse as "a heap of raw materials" (qtd. in Faas, 186). According to Ted Hughes, this dependence on rationalism whereby looking upon everything around as an object of consumption and domination has caused irreparable distortion and disruption in the modern man's experience. He believes that the Western man is succumbing to a suicidal evasion of nature, which alone constitutes what is "original and essential" (Underhill, 303) in the external as well as the internal world of man. His poetry exercises a particular fascination for the deep ecologists who argue that the modern man "needs to develop a value system which takes the intrinsic and inherent value of nature as the starting point" (Garrard, 18). Thus, he shifts the focus of the whole postmodern discourse from "human-centred to a nature-centred value, bringing it into opposition with Ted Hughes, in the true mode of deep ecology, stands at the threshold of the post-humanist tradition and the modern environmental discourse. He, in his poetry, tries to seek redemption not by turning into a hero or Superman, but by reducing himself to one of the simple living creatures on the existential plane. He sees man as "part of an organic universe, living best by acknowledging its wonders and rejecting the temptation to force his will upon it" (Session, 107). For Hughes "science, philosophy and religion are all themselves symptoms of the chronic, perhaps, terminal condition" and, thus, incapable of any redemptive possibilities for man. He, as a poet, takes upon himself to carry out the highly responsible task of restoring the primaeval dignity of man and the vision of sacredness and relevance to this existential play which has been disfigured beyond recognition on account of the dubious evolutionary march of mankind.

Globalization of capitalism with its manifesto of rapid expansions of the mechanistic forms of life and the consumerist culture has posed a grave threat to authentic living. But both these tendencies originating out of the basic existential dichotomy have evoked diverse and conflicting responses and have led to the creation of different varieties of ideology-oriented literature. There are some who seek a solution within the given conditions and plead for constant efforts towards "new forms of collective living" (Jameson, 181). But there are other groups distinguished by a stance of total rejection of the whole progression of the Western culture from the Renaissance onwards, finding nothing positive or acceptable in it. They believe, as do the deep ecologists and ecofeminists, that "the view put forward by, among others, Francis Bacon, Rene Descartes and Issac Newton represent the decisive blow to the organic universe" (Garrard, 61). They reject the practical philosophy of Descartes in which "knowing the force and action of fire, water, air, the stars, the heavens, and all other bodies that surround us he and his contemporaries might become "masters and possessors of nature" (49). Ted Hughes's world-view is in complete c sonance with the central contentions of the contemporary anthropologist Claude Levi Strauss who, as David Pace serves, is "opposed to the Faustian world of modern We ern civilization, where the balance between man and nature has been destroyed, where rapid change has eliminated all sense of proportion, and where the drive for power has over- whelmed the drive for harmony" (54). This 'evolutionary error', he contends, can be conveniently rectified by a return to nature. So, there is a constant desire throughout his poetry to go back to the 'origin', dropping all the conditioned responses of the cultural establishment. His writings, thus, exhibit a definitive affinity with the schools of thought and the traditions in literature which, as M.H. Abrams says, believe that the "ideal stage of man's way of life lies in the very distant past, when he lived naturally, simply and freely. and that the process of history has been a gradual 'decline' from that happy stage into increasing artifice, complexity inhibition and prohibitions in the psychological, social and cultural order" (138). His obsessive concern with nature as a source of some philosophical or 'protoreligious' significance offers an authentic panacea for all the warped complexities and distortions of the dilemmas of the post-Holocaust world. Consequently, his poetry actually offers some original and profound insights into modern man's predicament. His celebration of nature as the 'Mother Goddess of man- kind' and the 'Mother of all life is central to his persistent striving for an ingenious metaphysical system that becomes only partially clear, either in some later poems of his early phase or his latter poetic works where through various animals or physical processes nature is invested with strong spiritual overtones and is treated with mystic reverence and ecstasy.

The poetry of Ted Hughes in the first three collections The Hawk in the Rain, Lupercal and Wodwo is a significant deviant to the established poetic treatment of the man-nature relationship. By invoking the 'elemental energy through the bold use of animal imagery he invites his readers to enter into fresh and authentic relations with the non-human world around him. At the first look his main concern is to "identify and describe these energies, powers and presences of the non-human universe, not only in human terms but in their own, that is, in Nature's terms" (Sagar, 4). The discrepancy and the characteristic tension between these two descriptions make the most powerful, liberating as well humbling effect on the readers. These poems deplore as well as disrupt the modern man's confidence in his intellectual and rationalist mode of comprehending reality and lend credence to the role and place of the irrational or the instinctual as a diagnosis and healing. Like a religious adept he "puts aside the cluttering of the civilized consciousness, in order to be receptive to something 'Beneath' or 'beyond' that consciousness" (Underhill, 270). "Thought Fox", one of his earliest and best-known poems announces Ted Hughes's creative credo, his poetics:

> I imagine this midnight moment's forest:
> Something else is alive
> Beside the clock's loneliness
> And this blank page where my fingers move.
> Through the window I see no star:
> Something more near
> Though deeper within darkness
> Is entering the loneliness. (CP, 21)

Concentration, at midnight, is on 'something else' that is beyond the perceptive reality projected by ego. It is in this 'obscure something' that man must look for 'something else' which will give healing and meaning. No "Apollonian light of secular rational humanism" (Underhill, 270) will guide man through. Even the starlight promised by the transcendental philosophies is of no use since it is also the construct of man's arrogant intelligence, and thus a misdirection. The value of this midnight darkness for Hughes symbolizes luminosity as he himself said that "Poetry w to drag into the clean nakedness of the light" (qtd. in Fa 182) The poem is, as is generally recognized, about the "mind's creation of an imaginary fox which is also used symbolize the creative faculty of the artist" (King, 116). The total structure of the poem evolves organically through well-sustained and controlled tension between the human and the animal, and the rational and the irrational. Sitting at his desk in a lonely room late at night, the poet-person is privileged with the required absence of the 'stars': the emblems of the conscious and the rational thinking processes Thus, psychologically prepared to welcome the dethroning of intellect as the "physical seat of learning", (Bold, 56) the persona assumes a 'higher consciousness' when he suddenly becomes aware of "Something more near/Though deeper within darkness" (CP, 21):...with a sudden sharp hot stink of fox, It enters the dark hole of the head./The window is starless still, the clock ticks,/The page is printed. (CP, 21)

Ted Hughes's following statement which is of direct relevance to our discussion of "The Thought Fox" opens a new scope for the interpretation of the poem:

> There is the inner life, which is the world of final reality, the world of memory, emotion, imagination, intelligence, and natural common sense, and which goes on all the time, consciously or unconsciously, as the heart beat. There is also the thinking process by which we break into that inner life and capture answers and evidence to support the answers out of it. That process of raid, or persuasion, or ambush, or dogged hunting, or surrender, is the kind of thinking we have to learn and if we do not somehow learn it, then our minds lie in us like the fish in the pond of a man who cannot fish. (qtd. in Faas, 43-44)

The statement obviously tells a great deal about his manner of viewing the world and his concept of reality as something existent in the interior of the unconscious mind. Ted Hughes implicitly suggests recourse to ritualistic rehearsals or poetic revelations as viable means of tackling the present-day condition. The ultimate reality as conceptualized in "The Thought Fox" also serves to clarify the poet's failure to appreciate the contributions of Sartre, Kafka and Einstein who, like most of his civilized and rationalist poetic personae, have lost contact with "the elemental power circuit of the universe" or "primal impulse" (Hughes qtd. in Faas, 39), both of which are actually two versions of the poet's underlying idealist position.

This polarity and tension between animal and man, irrational and rational, vitality and death form the main pattern of Ted Hughes's poetry in all three collections. The very first poem "Hawk in the Rain" in his first book The Hawk in the Rain pitches the battle. The poem appropriately announces the major themes of Hughes's poetic journeyman in relation to animals, the earth, the weather, time and mortality, intellect and intuition. The poem opens with the existential dilemma of the persona:

> I drown in the drumming ploughland, I drag up Heel
> after heel from the swallowing of the earth's mouth,
> Each clay that clutches my each step to the ankle With
> the habit of the dogged grave... (CP, 19)

T in the poem is overwhelmed by the muddy earth which is acting like a violent beast, determined to devour him. Finding his anxiety-ridden state of consciousness un able to provide any stability, the persona gets a glimpse of an instinctually vibrant hawk. While he himself is totally at the mercy of the elements and flounders and struggles like prey already in the predator's mouth, he finds the hawk on a defiant and assertive level of existence. The wind, to which the hawk is responding quite differently, is also seen as antagonistic as the muddy earth:

> Thumbs my eyes, throws my breath, tackles my heart,
> And rain hacks my head to the bone, the hawk hangs
> The diamond point of will that polestars….

The poems like Egg Head, Fire Eater, Famous Poet, Meeting and Wind are a savage attack on the civilizational tendencies and evolutionary errors of the last three hundred years in the Western world. These poems subvert the rationalist modern man's confidence in his intellectual powers. The poems present a tragic spectacle of a wounded civilization that has alienated man from nature. In Egg-Head and Famous Poet Ted Hughes presents a virulent affront to the ordinary intellectuals of the world. (CP, 19) There are several poems such as October Dawn, Strawberry Hill,

"The Bear", "Ghost Crabs" and even one part of "Song of a Rat" which express the poet's conviction that the marginalized forces of nature are destined to regain a central place in the universe. "October Dawn" announces that the "ice- age had begun it heave" (CP, 37). "Song of a Rat" depicts the small creature as "attacking heaven and earth with a mouthful of screeches like tom tin" (CP, 169). Subsequently, all the physical agonies of the rat culminate with the elements around imploring it to be either alive or remain present in the universe as an unkillable and revengeful presence. Thus the rat, as a symbol, of "Crossing into power/Never to be buried" (CP, 169) becomes a symbol of wider implications. Elaborating this point, Stuart Hirsch- berg observes pertinently:

Amidst thunder and lightning the spirit of the rat... assumes domination over the universe. The irrational bestial forces freed by man's brutality and represented here in the character of the rat become a permanent presence and an active principle of evil in the world. As a result, the rat's spirit, 'supplants hell' by taking over Satan's task of making evil predominate. For Hughes, then, the new order... is a universe of implacable metaphysical evil arising from man's inhumanity and characterized by terror, violence and death. (58)

The Bear is a great mythical as well as mystical evo- cation: "In the huge, wide-open, sleeping eye of the mountain/The bear is the gleam in the pupil/Ready to awake" (CP, 160). In many cultures, bear is viewed as a mountain god. Sir James Frazer records in The Golden Bough that certain tribesmen, when asked about their origin, say "as for me I am a child of the god of the mountains. I am descended from the divine one who rules in the mountains", meaning as Frazer adds "no other than the bear" (qtd. in Hirschberg, 35). In Hinduism, one of the most Orientals of the world religions, the cosmic 'Kailash Parvat' is held in great reverence as a symbol of God Shiva, the God of destruction. Thousands of worshippers make pilgrimage to the place in the toughest of weather to pay obeisance to the God Kailash. Like

Kailash Mountain, the bear Hughes describes, is dormant, but he, in the dream, is contemplating about his relation with the human world. What one sees through the dream is the real resurrection of an evil and destructive spirit alms ready to pounce on everything and take it into his deadly embrace. Like the hawk half-asleep in "Hawk Roosting", the bear is in hibernation. The hawk's arrogant and anti-human demeanour was tactically defended by the poet saying that in this hawk Nature is thinking. The first-person narrative was essentially the foundation of this mythical logic. Simi larly "The Bear" too has been depicted as a symbol of nature and the poet intends to blame and forewarn egocentric and anthropological tendencies for this disastrous state of affairs where nature, driven to the corner by the rapacious culture, is trying to reclaim the lost space:

> The bear is digging
> In his sleep
> Through the wall of the Universe
> With a man's femur. (CP, 160)

And man, with all his science and technology, has to play the role of the prey and submit himself to this Almighty nature. The only course left and the only salvation possible from this wrath of nature, according to Ted Hughes, is in shedding the Faustus- like pride and establishing a genuine relationship with nature that lies in hibernation at his deeper instinctual level.

This tragic reality inherent in the creation of The Bear gains a sharp momentum in Ghost-Crabs. The poet commemorates the destructive potential of the invading natural and irrational forces ready to devour and annihilate everything that man can think of.

> They are the powers of this world. We are their bacteria,
> Dying their lives and living their deaths.....
> They are the turmoil of history, the convulsion
> In the roots of blood, in the cycles of concurrence. (CP, 150)

By making bold use of animal imagery Ted Hughes invites his readers to enter into new and fresh relations with the non-human world around him. Ted Hughes's poetry of this phase tends to be exhilarating and liberating in its at- tempt to reassert the role and place of the irrational or the instinctual in the highly mechanical forms of contemporary life. His recurrent concern with man's quest for negotiation with nature, as exhibited in the poems of The Hawk in the *Rain, Lupercal and Wodwo*, actually amounts to a romantic longing for a tension-free wholeness of being and simpler forms of social existence. The animal itself is invested with the nostalgia for a historically lost and elusive human world. Ted Hughes's poetry discussed above associates this primordial state of being with animal instinct, which in human beings has been hounded by the guardians of consciousness, of the super-ego who would reduce it to nothing at all. In the highly urbanized, industrialized and technocratic world of today afflicted with all kinds of severe tensions and conflicts which such a pattern of life carries within itself, and threatened by the ecological catastrophe and nuclear bombs, Ted Hughes's diagnosis and prescription infuse a new ray of hope for the renewal and re-invigoration of life on the face of the earth. His poetry of the early phase is thus an espousal and validation of the instinctual and intuitive mode for authentic living in full trust and acceptance of mother nature. Ted Hughes's deep ecology replaces the disastrous egocentric worldview of this post-modern culture with ecological ethics which alone can guarantee an authentic and unified existence on the face of mother earth.

Works Cited:

Abrams, M. H. A Glossary of Literary Terms. Madras: Macmillan, 1978.

Bold, Alan. Thorn Gunn and Ted Hughes. Edinburgh: Oliver and Boyd, 1976. Burke, Edmund. A Philosophical Enquiry into the origin of our ideas of the sublime and the beautiful. Oxford: Oxford UP, 1990. Descartes, R. 'A Discourse on Method', 'Meditations on the First Phi losophy' and 'Principles of Philosophy. London: Routledge,

1986. First published in 1637.
Garrard, Grey. Ecocriticism. London: Routledge, 2007. Gifford, Terry and Neil Roberts. Ted Hughes: A Critical Study.London: Faber, 1981.
Heidegger, Martin. M. Basic Writings. Ed. D.F. Krell. London: Rout ledge, 1993. Hirschberg, Stuart. Myth in the Poetry of Ted Hughes. Dublin: Wolf- hound P, 1981.
Hughes, Ted. Collected Poems (CP in the parenthesis). Ed. Paul Hagen. London: Faber, 2003.
Porter David. Beasts/Shamans/Baskin: The Contemporary Aesthet- ics of Ted Hughes. Critical Essays on Ted Hughes. Ed. Leonard M. Sciraj. New York: G.K. Hall & co
Bantis Stefano De Nature and Man: The Hindu Perspection. Varana Bociecos & Dilip Kumar Publishers, 1995. Schama 8. Landscape and Memory. London: Harper Collins, 1995
Schmidt Michael. An Introduction to the Fifty Modern British Pate London: Pan Book Ltd, 1979.
Schopenhaur, Arthur. The World as Will and Representation. Trans E.P.J. Payne. New York: Dover, 1969. Beiraj Leonard M. "Introduction" Critical Essays on Ted Hughes. B Leonard M. Beiraj. New York: G.K. Hall & Co., 1992.1-38.
West, Thomas. Ted Hughes. London: Methuen, 1985.

20. Gandhian Ideology in Literature: A Study of Raja Rao's *Kanthapura* & R K Narayan's *Waiting for the Mahatma*

Sunit Bhandari

Abstract: Mahatma Gandhi's steadfast struggle sought freedom in India and paved the way for the progress of the nation. Gandhiji's charismatic personality inspired and influenced people from all spheres of life. Scholars from varying disciplines like philosophy, history and literature dabbled in their distinctive styles to depict the aura and principles of Gandhiji. Indian English literature, too, was immensely impacted by Gandhiji's philosophy and great writers like Raja Rao and R K Narayan enriched Indian English literature with their prolific writings depicting Gandhian doctrines. Raja Rao's *Kanthapura* displays Gandhian ideology and his principles of nonviolence, truthfulness and ahimsa. The novel portrays Gandhiji as a national leader, as a divine incarnation to help the people break the shackles of slavery and free Mother India from the clutches of British rule. Raja Rao's artistic excellence and great craftsmanship are evident in showing Gandhi as an absent persona bringing life into the lifeless, illiterate and suppressed common masses of a remote small village 'Kanthapura'. R K Narayan in his novel *Waiting for the Mahatma* delineates Gandhi as a compassionate, straightforward forward and perceptive character whose ideology transforms a reckless fellow 'Sriram' into a patriotic, truthful and non-violent young man. The present paper intends to explore the different perspectives of these two writers in depicting Gandhian ideology as the power that built the nation and connected common people to him to be shown the right path like a beacon of light.

Keywords: Freedom, Nation and Gandhism.

Mahatma Gandhi's contribution to the freedom struggle is unsurpassable. No area of modern study has remained uninfluenced by Gandhian ideology. Education, philosophy, history, politics, economics, religion, social life, language & literature all have been greatly inspired and influenced by Gandhiji's distinctive perspectives. Writers from diverse spheres have depicted the aura and immaculate character of Gandhiji with their respective ingenuity. The distinct impact of Gandhi's ideology was visible in Indian English literature in the mid-1930s. Mulk Raj Anand, R K Narayan, Raja Rao, Manohar Malgonkar and many other writers enriched Indian English literature with their prolific writings relating to Gandhism and Gandhi era though drawing individual conclusions. Raja Rao and R K Narayan assiduously reconnoitered in their writings the Gandhian ideals of loving one's enemy, non-violence, satyagraha, the emancipation of women and eradication of untouchability. Both the writers portrayed Gandhi as a saint arousing national awakening with his non-violent struggle for the liberation of India. Raja Rao was greatly influenced by the Gandhian philosophy as he was a child of the Gandhian age. His novel *Kanthapura* was published in 1938 during the most turbulent times of the Indian freedom struggle movement led by Mahatma Gandhi. Those were the stirring days when Gandhi had already emerged as a national leader, assumed an all-India character, and become a motivating force in the social and political scenario of India. The novel displays Gandhian philosophy, his principles of non-violence, truthfulness and Swadeshi.

K.R. Srinivasa Iyengar appreciates this novel as "a Gandhi Purana than a piece of mere fiction" (391). It portrays Gandhi as a divine incarnation, a mythical figure to help the people come out from the chains of slavery and free Mother India from the clutches of British rule. Raja Rao's artistic excellence and great craftsmanship is apparent in presenting Gandhi as an absent hero/

persona bringing life into the lifeless, illiterate and curbed common masses of a small, remote, slumbering village *Kanthapura*, situated in South India on the Malabar coast.

The novel can be called a Gandhi Epic, the theme being the impact of Gandhi on the people of *Kanthapura*. *Kanthapura* is the microcosm of Indian traditional society as the events happening in *Kanthapura* were also happening in India during 1919-1930. The village suddenly awakens from inertia under the influence of the non-violent, non-cooperation movement of Gandhi.

Thus, Raja Rao tactfully incorporates Gandhian ideology with the theme of deplorable social and economic conditions of Indian villages. He gives us a peep into the values that saved the distressed masses from flood, fire, famine and exploitation both within and without. Gandhi's revolutionary ideas, ideals and practices during the freedom struggle electrified the entire nation to fight for the independence of India wielding the weapons of non-violence, passive resistance, non-cooperation and truthfulness. Raja Rao distinctly delineates the story of the resurgence of India under Gandhi's leadership.

The narrative develops in the form of a story told by a loquacious woman Achakka, a grandmother of *Kanthapura*. She is narrating things to a newcomer like a grandmother narrates stories to her grandchildren, mixing fact and fancy, history and myth. All the events of this freedom struggle movement are recorded in a conversational style and seen through the eyes of an elderly widow, through the sharp edges of her memory, sensibility and temperament. She is rendering endless tales of Gandhian business in a very lucid style long after the events have taken place (in which she had actively participated). Raja Rao's choice of oral storytelling of historical events helps in relating to the past and the impact of change. *Kanthapura* is a traditional caste-ridden village, far away from the modern style of living. The caste hierarchy is explicitly evident in the division of the Brahmin quarters and the Pariah quarters etc. The upper-class people maintain great distance from lower-caste people. The novel gives a detailed account of the poverty, exploitation and helplessness of the workers and the coolies working for very fewer wages in the Skeffington coffee estate. The Skeffington coffee estate stands as a symbol of cruelty, exploitation and inhumanity to which Indian people were subjected by British colonial power. Amid such social setup of caste, colour, creed, pride, prejudice and exploitation, the central character Moorthy is introduced "as a noble cow, quiet, generous, serene, deferent and Brahminic, a very prince" (*Kanthapura* 5). Patel Range Gowda, the village headman describes Moorthy as Gandhi of *Kanthapura*:

> He is our Gandhi. The state of Mysore has a maharaja, but that maharaja has another maharaja who is and that one has another one in heaven, and so everybody has his own Mahatma, and this Moorthy, who has been caught in our knees playing as a child, is now grown up and great, and he has wisdom in him and he will be our Mahatma... (*Kanthapura* 86).

Moorthy goes to the city and gets familiar with Gandhian philosophy. He becomes a staunch follower of Gandhiji. At the call of Mahatma, he leaves his studies and burns the foreign clothes along with other Gandhian followers. He dedicates himself entirely to the cause of the Gandhian movement. He starts campaigning against the inhuman practice of untouchability in the village. In the instance of Gandhiji, he mingles with pariahs and accepts milk from their hands though he is a high-class brahmin himself. He undergoes much suffering for being a Gandhian and satyagrahi. He is excommunicated by Swami and the villagers; he loses his mother who dies out of shock to see the excommunication of her son. Moorthy continues spreading Gandhi's progressive ideas of widow remarriage, women education and inspires the people to rise above the narrow-minded thinking of casteism.

Moorthy galvanizes the people to participate in the 'Don't Touch the Government campaign', Non-cooperation Movement, Civil Disobedience Movement and Dandi March. He propagates Gandhi's ideology of non-violence and truth and keeps on fighting against the injustice, inequality and cruelty of the Britishers. He educates the coolies. He does not react when he is beaten by Bade Khan, a representative of the Britishers. This shows how Moorthy has truly imbibed the spirit of Gandhiji. Some coolies have a scuffle with Bade Khan and Moorthy becomes sad. He undergoes penance and self-purification by following three days fast. He becomes an embodiment of Gandhian values and leads the villagers on a peaceful Satyagraha against the sale of toddy. He mobilizes the people to form a Congress committee. Every member of the Congress committee, it is decided, will practice ahimsa, speak the truth and spin the yarn. He gets arrested for taking part in the freedom struggle movement but all these things bring transformation in his character and he grows stronger spiritually.

Thus, the political theme gets highlighted by Gandhian ideals of truth, non-violence and non-cooperation. Gandhi is present in the background but he gives a constant point of reference to the narrative. Gandhi's spirit pervades throughout the novel. V. Srinivasa observes in this regard: "Though Gandhi does not figure as a character in action, the entire action of the novel is sustained by the spirit of Gandhi"(106). The motivating force of Gandhi's charismatic personality, the impact of his teachings, philosophy of life and political struggle is seen through the actions of the characters in this novel.

Advocate Shankar is also a true follower of Gandhi. He tries to take up true cases only, speaks the truth, wears khadi, and attends only that marriage where everyone is clad in khadi. He helps Moorthy in the freedom struggle movement and offers help when Moorthy is in jail. Gandhi's doctrines and philosophy are markedly discernible in the character of Sankar. Another important character who follows Gandhiji in truth and spirit is Rangamma. She takes charge of the freedom struggle movement in the absence of Moorthy when he goes to jail. She is really a very courageous and versatile woman who not only supports Moorthy throughout the narrative but also infuses strength among the ordinary women folk of the village. She inspires them by narrating tales of Rani Lakshmi Bai and Sarojini Naidu. She forms the 'Sevika Sangha' in the village and trains the women to bear the cruelties of the police peacefully. The women of the village too plunge wholeheartedly into this movement for freedom shouting slogans of 'Mahatma Gandhi ki Jai' and 'Inquilab Jindabad'.

Raja Rao has skillfully mingled religion and contemporary politics and Gandhian ideology is always the central point in every myth. Gandhiji is compared to Lord Shiva:

'Lord Shiva is three-eyed.... and Swaraj too is three-eyed: self-purification, Hindu Moslem unity, khaddar' (*Kanthapura* 11).

Again, Gandhiji is shown as an emblem of divine power and incarnation of lord Krishna killing the serpent of foreign rule. The novelist elevates the Gandhian movement with an allegorical connotation. Gandhi is presented as Lord Rama, the red foreigner as a soldier in Ravana's army, and Mother India as goddess Sita. Iyengar aptly observes, "Gandhi is the invisible God, Moorthy is the visible avatar. The reign of the red man is asuric rule, and it is resisted by the devas, the satyagrahis" (391).

Kanthapura is truly a great work of art. M. K. Naik rightly observes: "Raja Rao's *Kanthapura* (1938) is easily the finest evocation of the Gandhian age in Indian English fiction"(17). Raja Rao has given an authentic account of the regeneration and revival of the Indian masses under the able leadership of Gandhiji. No other book of independent or pre-independent India can give us such a realistic account of the Gandhian era. It is a wonderful social document depicting the impact of Gandhi on the common people.

R K Narayan is probably the most widely read novelist in Indian English. He along with Mulk Raj Anand and Raja Rao has contributed a lot to the development of the Indo-Anglican novel. He may be considered one of the few writers in India who take the craft seriously and are devoted to achieving the norms of perfection. He has produced many famous works including

Waiting for the Mahatma. Like Raja Rao in *Kanthapura*, Narayan too focuses on the role of Gandhiji as a political leader and philosophical guide. Gandhiji's personality was one of the modern influences that created a connection between the past and present culture of India. Himself an enigmatic man, he was a great force who provided the whole generation of Indians in pre-independent India a new sense of dignity, purpose and character. The masses were greatly influenced by Gandhiji's strong patriotism, ethical values, and asceticism. Spirituality has been a hallmark of India and Gandhi preached to the people to practice spirituality in their words and actions.

The novel *Waiting for the Mahatma* illustrates the influence of Gandhi's ideology and philosophy on people during the freedom struggle movement in India. It also covers the years of political turmoil and Gandhi as one of the leading characters with his doctrines of ahimsa, Satyagraha and non-violent resistance. The novel delineates Gandhi as a compassionate, straightforward forward and perceptive character whose ideology transforms a reckless fellow Sriram into a patriotic, truthful and nonviolent young man.

Waiting for the Mahatma starts when Sriram's grandmother gives him a savings passbook. First, there is a sudden rise in his fortune. Next, he experiences feminine beauty when he accidentally meets Bharati who is collecting funds for the Gandhian movement. Bharati is a powerful young heroine and a true Gandhian. Sriram falls in love with her and decides to live near her. Therefore, he attends the lecture delivered by Mahatma Gandhi and with his permission, starts working with Bharati. In company of Gandhiji, both of them visit different villages. The appalling village life gives an entirely different picture to Sriram but he keeps on working hard, spinning clothes, spreading the ideals and principles of Mahatma. Bharati promises to marry him if Gandhiji gives permission to both of them. Later, he comes in contact with Jagdish, a terrorist and supporter of I.N.A. He is arrested but even in jail, he does not lose his patriotic fervour and lofty ideals. Later after the departure of Britishers from Indian soil, Sriram is also released from jail. He hears that Gandhi is the new emperor. He is a changed soul now. He again meets Bharati who has always been a source of inspiration for him. It is Bharati who has brought him into the company of Mahatma and transformed Sriram into a patriotic and mature person. He again proposes to Bharati. They get permission from Bapuji but immediately after get the sad news of Gandhi's assassination.

It's a remarkable novel focusing on Gandhi's principles of truth and non-violence but Gandhiji seems to be a minor character in terms of his appearance in the novel. Sriram is the primary character through whose perspective the reader gets an insight into the narrative. The main intent of the novel focuses on the experiences of Sriram passing through the political turmoil to marry Bharati. Iyengar observes in this regard:

> Gandhiji is too big to be given a minor part.... on the other hand, he is sure to turn the novel into a biography if he is given a major part... In *Waiting for the Mahatma*, the theme is apparently the Bharati-Sriram romance which, however, gains a new dimension in the background of their common allegiance to Mahatma. (372)

Here we find two different perspectives. It would have been best for any contemporary writer to keep Gandhi in the background showing his influence indirectly. Raja Rao, the great craftsman, has kept Gandhi in the background exploiting the magic and name of his presence doing justice to the grand stature of Gandhiji. *Waiting for the Mahatma* stands apart. R K Narayan has presented Mahatma as a real character which is quite challenging observing the vigorous spirit of the persona himself.

But we appreciate the novel on the whole that it vividly describes the Gandhian mobilization, and various movements led by Gandhi before and after gaining freedom. However, it's worthwhile to go through Iyengar's observation:

> Since the stress is not merely on Gandhi's influence but on Gandhi himself—we see him in Malgudi stationed in

Nallappa's Grove and we see him, years later, in Delhi on his way to prayer on the fatal day, 30 January 1948—the novel develops a duality of interest which is not wholly resolved by the compulsion of art. *Waiting for the Mahatma* is an ambitious effort, and an impressive feat; but one also feels that Narayan's art—now denied the security of Malgudi and catapulted into Gandhian or terrorist political action—betrays unsureness and perplexity . . . It is Bharati who makes a patriot and a man of Sriram, and in marriage, he is certain to find in her the saviour strength that is woman's shakti (373).

Gandhiji is not a mere mortal but an ideology, a philosophy, an inspiration, an epitome of honesty, integrity, courage and dedication for all Indians. His persona is too large to be encapsulated even by such established writers as Raja Rao and R K Narayan. Gandhian presence as a person or Gandhian presence in absentia is different perspectives of these celebrated writers. However, the underlying connection is that almost every Indian writer has tried to weave narratives to espouse Gandhian ideology.

Works Cited:

Iyengar, K.R. Srinivasa. *Indian Writing in English*. New Delhi: Sterling Publishers Private Limited, 2009.

Naik, M.K. and Shyamala. A. Narayan. *Indian English Fiction: A Critical Study*. New Delhi: Pencraft Publication, 2009.

Rao, P. Mallikarjun and M. Rajeshwar, Ed. *Indian Fiction in English*. Srinivas, V. "Myth and Experiment in *Kanthapura*." New Delhi: Atlantic Publishers and Distributers,1999.

Rao, Raja. *Kanthapura*. Gurugram: Penguin Books, 2014.

LIST OF CONTRIBUTORS

- Swetha K, Assistant Professor (Journalism), St Claret College, Bangalore.
- Dr Jaideep Chauhan, Associate Professor, PG Dept of English, Sanatan Dharma College, Ambala Cantt.
- Dr Anshu Chaudhary, Assistant Professor, Dept of English, Gandhi Memorial National, Ambala Cantt.
- Mandeep Kaur, Research Scholar, MCM DAV College for Women, Punjab University, Chandigarh.
- Jaibhagwan Siwach, Assistant Professor, Dept of English, MPN College Mullana (Ambala)
- Jasleen Kaur, Research Scholar, MCM DAV College for Women, Punjab University, Chandigarh.
- Gulshan Kumar, Assistant Professor, PG Dept of English, Sanatan Dharma College, Ambala Cantt.

- **Dushruth Gutt, Assistant Professor, Dept of English, Govt College for Women, Sirsa.**
- **Dr Seema Gupta, Associate Professor, Dept of English, RKSD PG College Kaithal.**
- **Dr Nirmal Atri, Principal, Government College for Women, Karnal**
- **Dr Neena, Assistant Professor, Dept of English, Gandhi Memorial National College, Ambala Cantt.**
- **Dr Anuradha, Assistant Professor, Department of English, MDSD Girls College, Ambala City.**
- **Dr Suneela Sharma, Associate Professor, Department of Higher Education, Himachal Pradesh.**
- **Anuradha, Research Scholar, Dept of English, Kurukshetra University,**
- **Dr Atul Rasika Moudgil, Professor, Dept of English, Institute of Integrated & Hons. Studies, Kurukshetra University Kurukshetra**
- **Dr Balwan Singh, Associate Professor, Dept of English, Government College for Women, Karnal,**

- Subhash Singh, Assistant Professor, Dept of English, Dyal Singh College, Karnal.
- Rupinder Kaur, Assistant Professor, PG Dept of English, Sanatan Dharma College, Ambala Cantt.
- Meenakshi, Assistant Professor, Dept of Computer Science, Markanda National College, Shahabad (M)
- Shivani Dhawan, Assistant Professor, Dept of English, Gandhi Memorial National College, Ambala Cantt.
- Jaswinder Kaur, Assistant Professor, Dept. of English, SD College, Ambala Cantt
- Sunit Bhandari, Associate Professor, Dept of English, KVA DAV College for Women, Karnal.

❑❑❑